HISTORY
of the SCOTS
Book 2

Ian Ferguson

Oliver & Boyd

To Linda and Colin

Oliver & Boyd
Robert Stevenson House
1–3 Baxter's Place
Edinburgh EH1 3BB

A Division of Longman Group UK Ltd

© Oliver & Boyd 1988

ISBN 005 003993 8

First published 1988

Set in 11/13pt Bembo
Produced by Longman Group (F.E.) Ltd
Printed in Hong Kong

Acknowledgements

The author and publishers are grateful to those listed below for permission to reproduce the following:

Ashmolean Museum, Oxford, photograph: 58 (top); Duke of Atholl's Collection at Blair Castle, Perthshire, photograph: 89; Bibliothèque de l'Institut de France, Paris, photograph: 23 (top right); Bibliothèque National, Paris, photograph: 10; BBC Hulton Picture Library, photograph: 19; Trustees of the British Museum, photographs: 11, 16, 18, 23 (bottom), 41 (right), 54, 56 (top), 58 (bottom), 81, 90 (top); Photographie Bulloz, photograph: 23 (top); Edinburgh City Libraries, photographs: 53, 56 (bottom); Department of the Environment: Crown Copyright, photograph: 73; E.T. Archives, photographs: 12, 14, 15, 17; Lord Egremont, photograph: 38; Faculty of Advocates, photograph: 65 (left); Glasgow Museums & Art Galleries, photograph: 59; Her Majesty the Queen, photographs: 90 (bottom), 92; Her Majesty the Queen on loan to the National Galleries of Scotland, photograph: 21 (bottom); Dean and Chapter of Hereford Cathedral, photograph: 9; The Mansell Collection, photograph 86 (bottom right); National Galleries of Scotland, photographs: 35 (2 top), 36 (right), 41 (left), 44, 57, 60, 64, 71, 85, 86 (top left), 87 (two), 96, 97; Trustees of the National Library of Scotland, photographs: 29 (top left), 37, 80; National Museums of Scotland, photographs: 21 (3 top), 29 (bottom right), 57 (bottom), 69; Earl of Rosebery, photograph: 57 (top); Royal Commission on Ancient Monuments, Scotland, photograph: 76; Scottish National Portrait Gallery, photograph: 4 & 5; Daniel Shackleton, photograph: 65 (right); Mrs Sudlow & Council of the Scottish History Society, photograph: 55; Surgeons Hall, photograph: 28 (bottom); University of St Andrews, photograph: 35 (bottom); Weidenfeld & Nicolson Ltd, photographs: 42, 70, 84; Wellcome Institute Library, London, photograph: 28 (top); In a private Scottish Collection, photograph: 87 (right); Great Scot! Pictures, photographs: cover.

Illustrations and maps by Donald Harley and Jeremy Gower

Contents

COCHRAN JAMES III KENNEDY BOYD MARIE JAMES II JAMES I DONALD of ROTHESAY ALBANY DOUGLAS ROBER
ALBANY MARGARET of CREIGHTON LIVINGSTON JOANNA the ISLES ROBERT III BARBOUR II
DENMARK

Teachers' Notes

One of the distinctive features of this series is the extensive use of visual and written source material. Although teaching by means of such sources is not new, one of the most interesting and exciting developments is their growing use in the everyday teaching of history. If the purpose of history is to help people in the present to understand those in the past then sources provide an excellent means of allowing us to listen to the authentic voice of the past.

History can also offer another benefit. Young people can cultivate through the study of history an attitude of critical enquiry which will stand them in good stead throughout their lives. Looking at the achievements, failures and follies of the past can provide excellent experience and a perspective on the present. This is one of the reasons for the inclusion of Case Histories. They are there to widen and deepen young people's knowledge of the past. The Case Histories are not intended to be 'debunking' exercises. The whole intention behind them is to show that the great and the famous—and even the Scots!—are only human like the rest of us. Above all, the Case Histories can show that there is more than one version of any event.

Through the narrative and the evidence that is presented in these pages, students will learn to recognise the value of historical evidence and to draw conclusions from it. They will also develop understanding of similarity and difference, continuity and change over time—vital concepts for making sense of today's changing world.

I wish to thank all those teachers and pupils who have helped me by their advice, discussions and arguments in writing this history of the Scots. Any mistakes or infelicities are mine.

Ian Ferguson

I Moving Outwards

A Scotsman Sails the Atlantic

There is an old tale told of how in 1391 the Scottish Earl of Orkney, Henry Sinclair, sailed away from Scotland to search for new lands in the Atlantic. The tale comes from an old book called *The Voyages of the Venetian brothers Nicolo and Antonio Zeno*. Antonio went as captain of Sinclair's ship and after leaving Greenland they were driven westward for six days when:

> At last land was discovered . . . then some men went to the land in rowing boats, and not long afterwards returned and reported a country and a still better harbour.

He told how the people there seemed to them half-savage, sheltering themselves in caves.

Perhaps the Scotsman Sinclair did land in America a hundred years before Christopher Columbus set out from Spain to look for a 'New World' in 1492. What is more likely is that Sinclair made a mistake when he said he had sailed *from* Greenland and instead he sailed *to* that island. The tale of Sinclair, no matter how much truth there is in it, shows that men were already trying to find out more about the world beyond Europe long before Columbus.

An Early View of the World

If you look at the map on the page opposite you will see how most people imagined the shape of the world to be in Sinclair's time. The map is called the 'Mappa Mundi' (Map of the World) and was drawn in Hereford in England about 1280.

The mapmaker has placed Jerusalem in the centre of the world—perhaps you can guess why. How does the Mappi Mundi differ from a modern atlas? Notice that there are only three Continents marked on the Mappa Mundi.

Marco Polo

In 1271, a few years before the Mappi Mundi was drawn, Marco Polo the son of a merchant from Venice in Italy travelled all the way across Asia. The journey took him two years. For seventeen years he lived at the court of the Emperor of 'Cathay' or China. When he returned home to Venice he wrote about his travels and of what he had seen of the wonders and riches of Cathay. One of the strangest things he saw was paper money:

> . . . this paper currency is circulated in every part of the Great Khan's dominions [the Emperor's lands]; nor dare any person, at the peril of his life, refuse to accept it in payment. All his subjects receive it without hesitation, because, wherever their business may call them, they can dispose of it again in the purchase of merchandise they require, such as pearls, jewels, gold or silver.

This shows how different Chinese money was from European. In order for this system to work it was necessary for everyone in China to use paper money. Think how most people in Europe traded for goods at that time.

Silks and Spices

The two things which European merchants like Marco Polo valued above all were Chinese silks and Asian spices. Already the Venetians were buying these and other Asian goods in the markets of Alexandria and other ports of the Eastern Mediterranean. Naturally, the Venetians tried to stop other European merchants from sharing in this rich and profitable trade.

Tall Tales

Only a few people read about Marco Polo's travels but many more read the *Travels* of Sir John Mande-

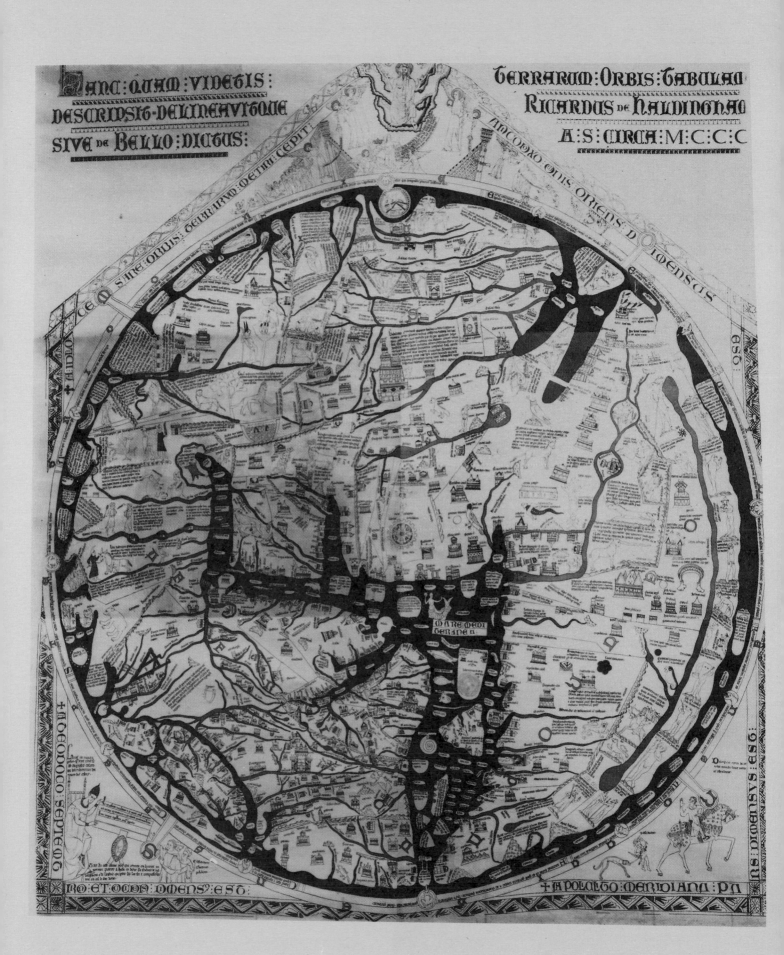

ville. Though they were very popular, the tales were untrue for Mandeville wrote down all the 'tall tales' he heard from travellers without ever visiting the countries he wrote about. Among many other wonderful things, the *Travels* described people whose heads were in their chests, like in the drawing above. Mandeville wrote this about Abyssinia (Ethiopia) in Africa:

> In this land ships are made without nails or iron bands because there are rocks of Adamant [magnetic iron] in the sea which would draw the ships on to them.

Ptolemy's Map: A Round World

The men who made the Mappa Mundi believed the Earth was flat. If you look at the map on the page opposite you will see how much the cartographers, or map-makers, had learned by 1482.

Surprisingly enough, this map was not based on the voyages of travellers but was a fifteenth-century copy of a map made 1300 years before by a Greek called Ptolemy. Ptolemy's map was one of the many things the men of the Renaissance times discovered from studying the writings of the Greeks and Romans. There are a number of differences between this map and the Mappa Mundi.

Prince Henry's Crusade

In 1415 the Portuguese captured the port of Cueta in Morocco. A Portuguese Prince, Henry the Navigator, encouraged seamen to use Cueta as a base to explore the west coast of Africa. He wanted to find new lands for Portuguese merchants to trade with. He also wanted to persuade other nations to join in a great Crusade against the Muslims. Henry thought the best way to do this was to convert people to Christianity. So you can see that these early explorers were as anxious to spread Christianity as they were to trade for gold, silk and spices.

10

The Portuguese gradually explored the west coast of Africa until Bartholomew Diaz rounded the Cape of Storms in 1487. The Portuguese King thought that this was an unlucky name and so he rechristened it 'The Cape of Good Hope'.

Da Gama Reaches India

Ten years later another Portuguese, Vasco Da Gama, sailed round the Cape and northwards up the east coast of Africa. He named one place 'Natal' for he sighted it on Jesus's Birthday, Natal Day. He continued sailing northwards until he reached the port of Malindi. There he was lucky enough to find a pilot who knew the safest way to sail across the Indian Ocean to Calicut on the south-west coast of India. Among his crew Da Gama had several convicts who had been set free on condition that they joined the expedition. Da Gama was not sure how the ruler of Calicut would greet him so he sent one of the ex-convicts instead of going himself! The Indians asked the convict what he had come for and he replied, 'We have come to seek spices and Christians'. With these words the convict summed up the whole reason for the voyage. When Da Gama finally returned to Lisbon two years later he had on board a cargo of cinnamon and pepper which paid for the cost of the voyage several times over. Pepper was particularly prized in the days before refrigeration.

Da Gama had shown Europeans how to sail directly to India and return with the spices they so desired. They no longer had to depend upon Muslim merchants for these luxuries. But the Portuguese were unwilling to share their discoveries and so other European sailors had to try and find their own ways to reach India and the East.

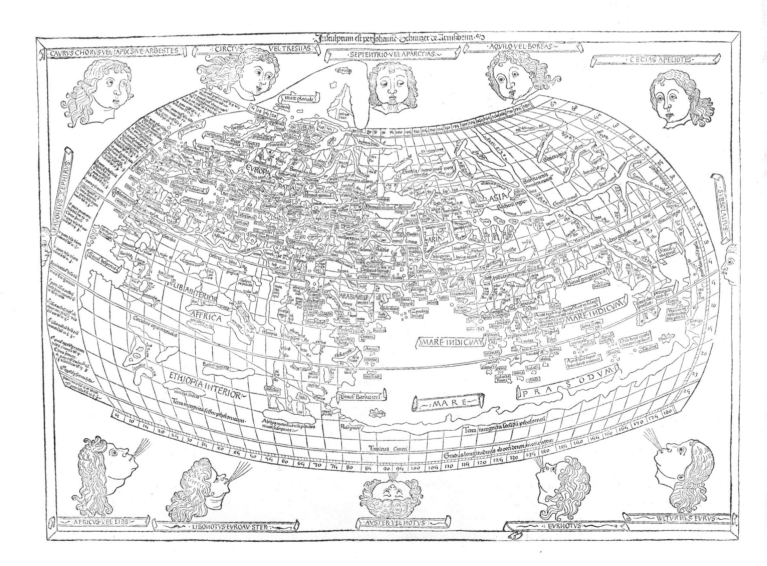

Caravels and Cogs

Look at the pictures on the page opposite. They show a Portuguese 'caravel' and an English 'cog'. The caravel was more difficult to handle in bad weather. The simple, square-sailed cog was better suited for the stormy northern seas.

The caravel's triangular sail helped to keep the ship on course and later on shipbuilders built larger ships called 'galleys'. These galleys were manned by oars-men who were often convicts.

Early Navigation

We know that the Mediterranean sailors found their way along its coasts by studying maps called 'portolans'. If you look at the portolan below you will see that the lines give compass directions from one place to another as well as the distances between these two places.

The sailors in northern waters could not rely on portolans as fogs, tides and stormy seas often made it difficult for them to see where they were. Instead, they relied mainly on compasses which told them the direction they were sailing. When they were in shallower water they could often tell quite closely where they were by the use of the leadline to tell them how deep the water was and if the sea-bed was sandy or rocky. There is a picture on this page of a sailor 'swinging the lead'.

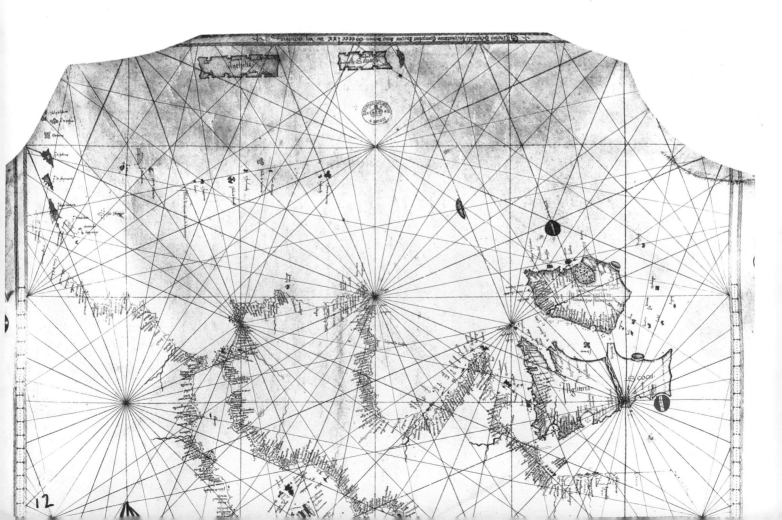

A Caravel

A Cog

ceanica Classis

The *Santa Maria*

A New Way to India

The Portuguese stopped other nations using the Cape route to India, so their explorers sought new ways to the East. One of these was Christopher Columbus who was born in Genoa in Italy. He had made many voyages round the coasts of Europe as far as Iceland. Columbus studied Ptolemy's map and worked out that if a ship sailed westward from Europe it would eventually reach China or India. Remember, neither Columbus nor Ptolemy knew of America for both thought the world was much smaller than it actually is. Columbus tried to sell his idea to the Portuguese but you can probably guess why they were not interested. Finally, Isabella, the Queen of Spain, gave him the money he needed and he set sail from Palos in south-west Spain on 3 August 1492. Under his command were three ships. The largest of them was his flagship, the *Santa Maria*.

Columbus made good speed into the Atlantic for the winds in that part of the world blow steadily to the west. As they sailed further into unknown waters Columbus tried to quieten the fears of his crew. Here is an extract from his log or journal:

> *Sunday, 9th September*
> This day the Admiral [himself] calculated that we had run [travelled] 19 leagues [122 kms] but he decided to record less than this number so that the crew would not be disheartened and terrified if the voyage was of long duration.

Do you think Columbus was right to tell his crew lies?

The New World

As the days passed the crew became uneasy and demanded he should return to Spain. Columbus finally agreed to do this if they did not sight land within two or three days. Luckily, two days later on Friday, 12 October 1492 they sighted an island which Columbus named Salvador. When Columbus saw the natives there he was sure he had reached Asia and he called them 'Indians'. He wrote about them:

> They would make good, intelligent servants for I observed they quickly took in what I said to them, and I believe that they could easily become Christians as they appear to have no religion.

Remember one of the reasons for Da Gama's voyage. It would seem that Columbus was already thinking of enslaving these people.

Columbus was disappointed because he did not meet the Emperor of China but after the 'Indians' had given him some tiny gold ornaments he was even more certain that he had reached an island off the coast of Asia. He wrote, 'I intend to go and see if I can find the island of Cipangu [Japan]'. Until he died in 1506 Columbus thought he had found islands off the coast of China.

The Naming of America

Many other explorers followed Columbus and they soon doubted his belief that he had reached Asia. One of them, Amerigo Vespucci who came from Florence, said that Columbus had discovered a 'New World'. Vespucci claimed to have made so many discoveries in this new world that the map-makers named it after him—'America'.

Aztecs and Incas

Later, explorers discovered the rich lands of Central and South America. Spanish soldiers, equipped with

The Spaniards landing in Mexico

weapons such as guns and horses which the native peoples had never seen before, conquered the Aztecs of Mexico and the Incas of Peru. By 1534 the Spaniards ruled a great empire in the New World, rich in gold and silver. This great wealth made Spain the greatest power in Europe.

Magellan's Voyage

By 1519 the Spaniards had not yet found the riches of the Americas and were still seeking ways to find the spice islands of Asia. In that year King Charles of Spain appointed the Portuguese Ferdinand Magellan to find a new way of reaching the richest spice islands of Molucca in modern Indonesia. Magellan was certain he would reach them by sailing southwards around America and then westwards until he reached East Asia.

He navigated his little fleet through the stormy Straits which are named after him and wrote: 'We came out of the strait into the Pacific Sea'. He called it this because it was peaceful after the Magellan Straits. For three months they sailed across the Pacific. They suffered many hardships for, like Columbus, Magellan thought the world was smaller than it is. His supplies began to run out. Finally, they reached the island of Cebu in the Philippines where Magellan persuaded the King to become a Christian and swear loyalty to the King of Spain. Shortly afterwards Magellan was killed fighting a battle for the King of Cebu.

Magellan's ship *Victoria* finally struggled home to Spain by the Cape of Good Hope, carefully avoiding all the Portuguese ports. The *Victoria* reached Spain nearly three years after it had departed and only 35 out of the original crew of 280 survived the voyage.

Drake Sails Round the World

It was nearly fifty years before another sailor, Sir Francis Drake, sailed round the world. In fact Drake only set out to plunder some of the King of Spain's ships. In 1577 he sailed through the Magellan Straits and attacked and captured some Spanish ships off the coast of Peru. Drake knew that if he tried to return the same way that he had come the Spaniards would be waiting for him. He decided to sail northwards up the west coast of America. At one place in what is now California he left a metal sign claiming the land for Queen Elizabeth I of England. He then sailed across the Pacific to the Spice Islands and from there round the Cape back to England. When he arrived home he had only one ship left of the original five. He had been forced to sail around the world to avoid the Spaniards. The Queen rewarded him with a knighthood for she was delighted to receive a part of the treasure he had looted from the Spaniards.

Other Ways to the East

Spain's wealth from the New World made the rulers and merchants of other European countries very envious. What added to their envy was the way the Spaniards and Portuguese prevented others from using their routes. Look at the map of the world on the page opposite. You will probably be able to find other ways of sailing to East Asia apart from those round Cape Horn and the Cape of Good Hope.

There were two possible ways open to them; to the north-east and the north-west. One lay along the northern coast of Russia and then into the north Pacific. The other was by the north of Canada and again into the north Pacific. So English, French and Dutch explorers began to search for these passages.

The North-west Passage

As early as 1497 Henry VII of England had sent John Cabot, a Genoese like Columbus, to explore the land north of Spanish America and claim any lands for England. When Cabot returned he had claimed 'New Found Land' as the first English colony in America. Although he did not find gold or spices Cabot did find other treasures for the seas off Newfoundland were one of the richest fishing grounds in the world!

Later the English sent other expeditions under Sir Martin Frobisher, William Baffin and Henry Hudson all of which failed to open up the North-west Passage and they left only their names on the maps. The picture below of a skirmish with Eskimos was drawn by John White who went with Frobisher's expedition of 1577.

The North-east Passage

The English and the Dutch also tried to find a North-east Passage and you can see from the picture on the page opposite the kind of hut they built to spend the long winter months in. Notice the lamp in the room, what kind of fuel would they use for it?

Jenkinson's Journey

In 1557 an English merchant, Anthony Jenkinson, sailed round the north coast of Norway to the Russian port of Archangel in the White Sea. He then made the dangerous journey to Moscow where he met Ivan the Terrible, the ruler of Russia. He carried on his journey by the River Volga until he reached the Caspian Sea. From there he travelled across Asia until he reached the great market city of Bokhara a meeting place for all the caravan routes of Central Asia:

> There is a great yearly resort [journeying] of merchants to this city who travel in great caravans [groups of merchants] from countries such as India, Persia, Russia and many other countries.

You can probably guess what kind of transport these merchants would use and what kind of goods they might sell.

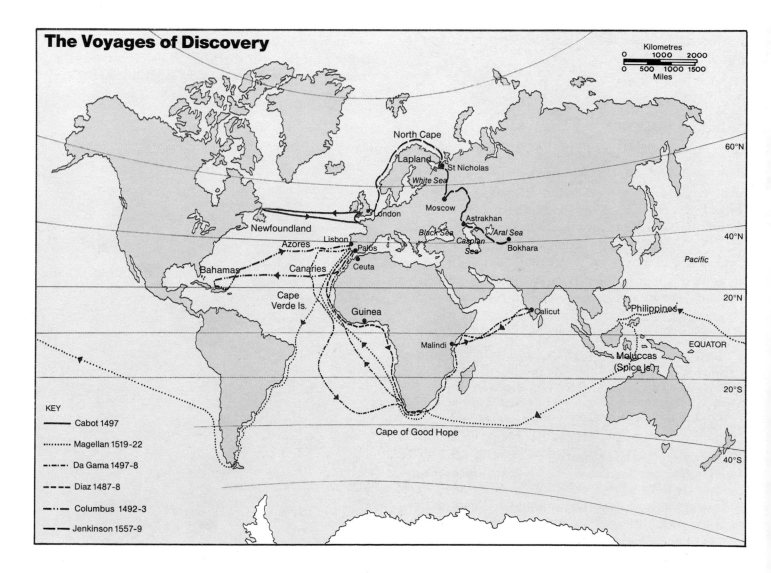

The Voyages of Discovery

Kilometres
0 1000 2000
0 500 1000 1500
Miles

North Cape
Lapland
St Nicholas
White Sea
Moscow
London
Newfoundland
Astrakhan
Black Sea
Aral Sea
Caspian Sea
Bokhara
Lisbon
Azores
Palos
Bahamas
Canaries
Ceuta
Pacific
Cape Verde Is.
Guinea
Calicut
Philippines
Malindi
EQUATOR
Moluccas (Spice Is.)
20°S
Cape of Good Hope
40°S

60°N
40°N
20°N

KEY
——— Cabot 1497
········· Magellan 1519-22
–·–·– Da Gama 1497-8
– – – Diaz 1487-8
–··–··– Columbus 1492-3
—— Jenkinson 1557-9

Though the English had found a kind of Northeast route to the East they did not follow it up. Instead they found other lands to explore and colonise. In 1600 some English merchants had formed the East India Company to trade with India and the Far East and were successful in taking over the trade of the Portuguese.

Settlements in the New World

The English went to America mainly as settlers. In 1585 Sir Walter Raleigh landed on Roanoke Island and left some settlers there. Soon other English settlers made the long and dangerous voyage to set up settlements along the east coast of North America. The most famous of those early settlers were the Pilgrim Fathers who landed at New Plymouth in 1620. Gradually these settlers took over the lands of the Red Indians and forced them to move further and further west. There was often much bitter fighting because the Indians resented the white men taking over their hunting grounds.

Great Dangers

You have seen the great losses of ships and men these early explorers suffered. Although many sailors drowned at sea or were killed by unfriendly natives, most died of disease. The sickness they feared most of all was scurvy. We know now that scurvy was caused by a lack of the vitamins contained in fresh fruit and vegetables. In those days they had no way of stopping food from rotting in warm weather and one of the reasons why spices were so widely used was to disguise the taste of rotten meat. One seaman who had suffered from scurvy wrote:

> It rotted all my gums which gave out a black and putrid [evil-smelling] blood. My thighs and lower legs were black and gangrenous [rotting] and I was forced to use my knife each day to cut into the flesh in order to release the black and foul blood.

Later explorers such as Captain Cook made their sailors drink lemon juice which prevented them from getting scurvy.

Making sure the sailors had enough food was another great problem. Sea captains had to take sufficient food for long sea voyages. Water stored in bar-

rels soon became stagnant. Bread went mouldy and even the hard ship's biscuit, though it did not become stale:

> ... was so light that when you tapped it on the table it fell almost to dust and thereout [out of it] numerous insects called weevils crawled: they were better to the taste ... if instead of these weevils large maggots with black heads made their appearance, then the biscuits were only considered to be in the first stage of decay.

Still the biscuits were eaten eagerly by the hungry sailors. When Magellan was crossing the Pacific even rats fetched a high price with his starving crew!

'To See Ourselves as Others See Us'

Most Europeans considered the natives of the countries they visited only fit to be slaves. The natives often had just as low an opinion of the Europeans. You can see from the picture on this page what Africans thought of the Portuguese with their large noses. On the page opposite there is an illustration showing what the Chinese thought of the British who had so much hair.

All Europeans were considered dirty by the Japanese for they rarely took the hot baths which the Japanese loved. The Chinese also looked upon the Europeans with contempt for the Chinese considered them ignorant and ill-mannered. Ugliest of all were those Europeans with red hair and blue eyes!

'Old Hairy One'.
How the Chinese saw a British sailor

Exchanges: Good and Bad

The Europeans left their mark on the lands they conquered or colonised. The descendants of the natives and Europeans learnt European languages like English, French, Spanish and Portuguese. They had to learn how to use European weapons but many did not learn quickly enough before they were conquered.

To the Americas the Europeans brought horses, cattle, pigs, sheep and goats. They also brought unpleasant things such as influenza and measles. In fact European diseases killed more American Indians than European bullets ever did.

The Europeans received much in return. They went in search of spices and brought back pepper, nutmegs, cloves and many others. The gold and silver they seized flowed in from Mexico and Peru and filled the Spanish treasury. From Spain gold and silver coins went to all parts of Europe. There had never been so many precious coins circulating before and this caused inflation. From the Americas we also received potatoes, tobacco, maize and beans. We still enjoy the Aztec 'choclatl'.

19

Something to Remember

The great voyages of discovery of the fifteenth and sixteenth centuries were above all for trade and religion. The explorers set out to find new people to trade with or new ways of travelling to the riches and spices of the East.

The Portuguese were the first to explore the east and west coasts of Africa and reach India and the East by the Cape of Good Hope route. The discovery of America by the Europeans can be seen as just another attempt to find a way to East Asia. Further explorers were in their turn trying to seek out new passages to the East because the Portuguese and Spaniards were determined to stop foreigners using their routes.

The voyages themselves were made in ships which were tiny to our eyes. These explorers suffered many hardships on the long voyages for they were faced with many dangers from the seas, hostile natives and, not least, from diseases like scurvy.

The results of the voyages were seen in many parts of the world. The language of Brazil is a dialect of Portuguese for the Portuguese explored and conquered Brazil. Today, the chief language of South and Central America is Spanish which shows where Spanish explorers, conquerors and settlers made their mark. English is the chief language of North America because these lands were first settled by English-speaking people. More than lands were discovered by the Europeans; new foodstuffs such as the potato were to change completely the eating habits of the whole population of Europe.

Something to Think About

The voyages of discovery changed the lives and thoughts of the people of Europe. Over the years millions of emigrants left their homelands to settle down and found new nations. They took much from their homelands but they and their children also changed their original languages and customs.

The weapons of the Europeans and their ways of waging war were better than most of the people they faced. The Europeans came first to trade and quickly realised they could easily defeat the natives of these countries. Soon the Spanish, Portuguese, English, French and Dutch had built up great empires in the Americas, Africa and Asia. First came the traders, then the soldiers and finally the governors. Because they had superior weapons the Europeans thought they were superior people. As skin colour was the easiest way of telling the difference between a European and a 'native' many Europeans began to imagine that having a 'white' skin was the sign of their superiority.

As many of the European conquerors had the habit of enslaving those who gave into them, the idea soon spread among Europeans that all the 'coloured' peoples were only fit to be the 'white' man's slaves. When ideas like 'white is best' and 'coloured slavery' are put together then you have racism—one of worst results of the 'moving outwards' of Europe.

A Rebirth of Knowledge

Kings and Coins

The three coins shown on this page are of an old Scottish coin called a 'groat' which was worth 4d (2p). The groat on the left-hand side which was made or minted between 1390 and 1406 shows the face of Robert III, the great-grandson of Robert the Bruce. The coin in the middle was minted in the reign of Robert III's grandson, James II, in about 1452. The right-hand groat was coined in 1485 during the reign of James III, James II's son. If an archaeologist discovers coins in a dig he can take them to an expert on coinage who can often date the coin precisely. In this way the archaeologist finds yet another way of dating the site. You can see that the historian would be able to use coins in the same way though you might remember from Book 1 that he would need to take great care when he did this.

Comparing Faces

Take a closer look at the groats. Do you see any differences in the way the Kings' faces are drawn? Notice that the face on the groat of James III looks different from the other two. The faces of Robert III and James II look the same, even though they are of grandfather and grandson. On this page there is also a painting of James III which is in the National Gallery of Scotland in Edinburgh. If you compare the portrait and the coin you can see that they are similar, in other words, they are the face of an *individual* person. Before James III's reign all the faces of Scottish kings on their coins looked alike. An expert on Scottish coinage described the portrait on James III's groat as:

> . . . the first true royal portrait on the Scottish coinage [and] is probably the earliest Renaissance coin portrait outside Italy.
>
> (Ian Halley Stewart, *The Scottish Coinage*, Spinks and Son, London, 1955, p. 67.)

The 'Renaissance'

The 'Renaissance' is the name which historians use to describe the fifteenth century in Europe when artists, astronomers, sculptors, architects, writers, teachers and scientists began to study the ideas of the Greeks and Romans. As they did so their own ideas about the world also began to change. The word, 'Renaissance' means a 'rebirth' of knowledge.

Questions and Answers

The scholars and artists began to question their old beliefs about the world and the answers they got from the writings of the Greeks and Romans seemed more true than those which were common in the fifteenth century. These Renaissance answers naturally upset many people who refused to listen to them. For example, Renaissance astronomers upset the old belief that God had placed the Earth at the centre of the Solar System. The old idea was that the Sun, Moon, Planets and Stars revolved around the Earth. An astronomer called Copernicus showed that this was not so and that the Sun was the centre of our planetary system of which the Earth was just one planet. It is easy to understand why so many people did not believe Copernicus and continued to believe the evidence of their own eyes.

Learning from the Greeks and Romans

One of the most exciting things that Renaissance scholars learnt from the Greeks and Romans was how to paint faces which looked like real human beings and to carve statues whose bodies looked like real human bodies. In Italian cities such as Rome and Florence artists saw proof of this as they studied the remains of Roman buildings and statues that were being dug up there. One nobleman from Florence who was visiting Rome in 1434 said,

> There are many splendid palaces, houses, tombs and temples . . . but all are in ruins.

These buildings might have been in ruins and the statues broken but to men of the fifteenth century they looked very different from those of the last few centuries. For one thing, the Greek and Roman statues were more *life-like* than the statues of the Middle Ages—that is, the statues of the Ancient World looked like real people. In fact, the men of the Renaissance felt much closer to the Greeks and Romans than they did to people of the Middle Ages, those who had lived between them and Ancient Times. The Renaissance men were rather contemptuous of the Middle Ages which they regarded as ignorant and superstitious times. They also thought that nothing much of importance had happened during the Middle Ages.

The Universe Before Copernicus

Stars

Sun

Moon

EARTH

Planets

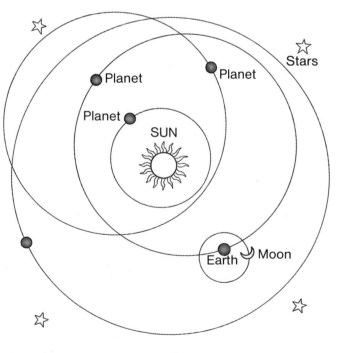

The Universe After Copernicus

Planet

Planet

Planet

SUN

Stars

Earth Moon

Leonardo Da Vinci

One great Renaissance man was Leonardo da Vinci (1452–1519). His biographer, Giorgio Vasari, described him like this:

> In appearance he was striking and handsome, and his magnificent presence brought comfort to the most troubled soul. He was so persuasive that he could bend other people to his will. He was so physically strong that he could withstand any violence; with his right hand he would bend the iron ring of a doorbell or a horseshoe as if it were lead. He was so generous that he sheltered and fed all his friends, rich or poor, provided they were of some talent or worth.

This sounds like over-praise but Leonardo was undoubtedly an all-round genius. He was an artist, an engineer and a scientist. He was like a giant with one foot in the world of art and the other in the world of science. He kept note-books filled with his own secret writing. He wrote down his ideas and inventions and drew pictures to explain them. Once he wrote:

> Iron rusts from disuse; stagnant water loses its purity and in cold weather becomes frozen; even so does inaction sap the vigour of the mind.

Think what Leonardo meant by this.

The First Helicopter

Leonardo's restless mind searched deeply into many things. He planned towns and fortified them. He made drawings of flying machines, including the first helicopter as you can see from the drawing above.

He drew plans of another machine and wrote beside it:

> I will make covered cars, safe and unassailable . [not able to be attacked] . . . which enter among the enemy.

You have probably already worked out what we call this war machine today. Leonardo was a mathematician, a physicist and a botanist. He studied plants and made drawings of them after he had dissected or cut them up. He also dissected human and animal bodies to study their anatomy. He then used his studies of human anatomy in his paintings which show bodies which have bones, tissue and muscle under their skins.

Leonardo's
armoured car

The Mona Lisa

Leonardo's painting, the 'Mona Lisa', is perhaps the best-known painting in the world. Vasari wrote:

> Leonardo subtly reproduced every living detail. The eyes had their natural brightness and moistness ... the eyebrows were completely natural, growing thickly in one place and lightly in another ... The mouth, joined to the flesh-tones of the face by the red of the lips, appeared to be living flesh rather than paint ... those who saw it were amazed to find that it was alive as the original [person].

Leonardo's work shows us how many different things the men of the Renaissance were interested in. Some studied Greek and Roman maps and learnt that the world was a globe and not flat as was commonly believed. The map they mostly studied was Ptolemy's which they used as a starting point for their own maps. You have seen how these Renaissance maps were used in the great voyages of discovery which began in the fifteenth century.

The Renaissance Prince

It was not only artists and scientists who were interested in reviving Greek and Roman knowledge. Rulers and princes admired the power and might of the Roman Empire and they employed Renaissance architects and artists to build them palaces in imitation of the Roman Emperors. Other European rulers also became patrons of Renaissance artists. Instead of only painting religious scenes as the artists of the Middle Ages had done, the Renaissance artists painted rulers, merchants and scenes from Greek myths and legends. Man became as important a subject as God.

All these works were intended to glorify European rulers and to show their subjects how powerful their rulers were. Everybody used coins and the ruler whose head was on the coin was showing how widespread his power was—as James III did.

A Turning Point

The Renaissance marks a turning point in human history. With the knowledge of the Greeks and Romans people began to question old beliefs. New translations of the Bible from the original Greek led people to doubt the authority of the Catholic Church. There were great advances in art and architecture. People began to use their eyes and minds to investigate the world instead of simply believing what they were told. Though Leonardo was outstanding in so many ways he is typical for his restless enquiring mind which made Man the measure of all things to the Renaissance people.

Son Fights Father

On 11 June 1488 the army of Prince James fought a battle at Sauchieburn against King James III, the Prince's father. A few months before some nobles had kidnapped the Prince and persuaded him to be their leader against James III with whom they were dissatisfied. The young Prince agreed as long as no harm came to his father. James III was defeated and as he fled from the battlefield he was thrown from his horse. As he lay injured in the mill at Bannockburn a stranger, pretending to be a priest, entered and stabbed the King to death.

Prince James was crowned King James IV at Scone on 25 June 1488. After his coronation it was said that he felt so guilty for causing his father's death that he wore a belt with iron weights on it. On every anniversary of Sauchieburn he would add another weight as a penance.

KINGS & QUEENS OF SCOTLAND 1307-1603

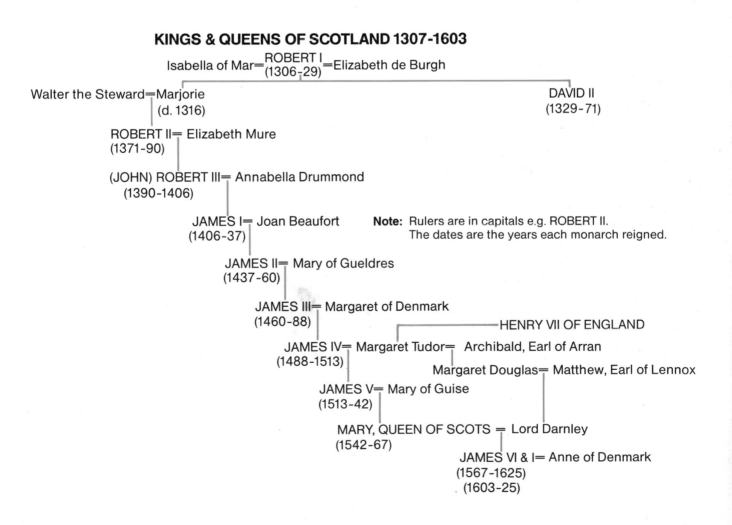

Isabella of Mar = ROBERT I (1306-29) = Elizabeth de Burgh

Walter the Steward = Marjorie (d. 1316)

DAVID II (1329-71)

ROBERT II = Elizabeth Mure (1371-90)

(JOHN) ROBERT III = Annabella Drummond (1390-1406)

JAMES I = Joan Beaufort (1406-37)

Note: Rulers are in capitals e.g. ROBERT II. The dates are the years each monarch reigned.

JAMES II = Mary of Gueldres (1437-60)

JAMES III = Margaret of Denmark (1460-88)

HENRY VII OF ENGLAND

JAMES IV = Margaret Tudor = Archibald, Earl of Arran (1488-1513)

Margaret Douglas = Matthew, Earl of Lennox

JAMES V = Mary of Guise (1513-42)

MARY, QUEEN OF SCOTS = Lord Darnley (1542-67)

JAMES VI & I = Anne of Denmark (1567-1625) (1603-25)

The New King

The young King was only fifteen years old. He had red hair, was very athletic and one of the best horsemen in all Scotland. It was said that he had once ridden all the way from Stirling to Aberdeen and then on to Elgin (that is over 300 kms) all in one day! Sometimes he fought in tournaments, a very dangerous pastime in which contestants were often injured or killed. Above all, he loved hawking and was supposed to have paid £180 for a single hawk—a vast sum of money for those days.

James was full of curiosity. He was fascinated by the new discoveries being made in Europe at that time. He wanted to find out for himself how to make guns and build ships. He ordered warships for the first Royal Scottish Navy. He wanted to find out what language children spoke if they had no one to copy —some wise men told him it was Hebrew, the language of Adam and Eve. He had two infants and a dumb nurse put on the island of Inchkeith but the only sounds the children made were those of animals and birds! Once he even gave money to a man who experimented in how to make gold out of lead.

Like other rulers of his time James was also interested in building. He improved his palaces at Stirling and Linlithgow and built a hunting palace at Falkland. He also built a new palace at Holyrood which was ready in time for his wedding in 1503.

The Spanish ambassador to Scotland, Pedro de Ayala, who was a very shrewd observer wrote this about James IV:

> He is courageous, even more than a King should be . . . I have often seen him undertake most dangerous things. On such occasions he does not take the least care of himself. He is not a good Captain because he begins to fight before he has given his orders.

It is true that James would often rush into danger, but his reply to de Ayala is worth considering:

> He [James] said to me that his subjects serve him with their persons and their goods, in just and unjust quarrels, exactly as he likes, and that therefore he does not think it right to begin any warlike undertaking without himself being the first in danger.

James was intelligent and picked up languages quickly. Here is de Ayala again:

> He speaks the following foreign languages: Latin, very well, French, German, Flemish, Italian and Spanish . . . his own Scottish language is as different from English as Aragonese is from Castilian. The King speaks, besides, the language of the savages who live in some parts of Scotland and the Islands.

Aragonese and Castilian are two dialects of the Spanish language and Ayala is saying that the Scots and English speak two different dialects of the 'English' language. James IV was probably the last Scottish King to speak Gaelic.

The Lord of the Isles

De Ayala might have regarded the Highlanders as 'savages' but James was determined to make them part of his kingdom. He did not want to share power with any other rulers in Scotland, but in the Highlands the 'Lord of the Isles' thought of himself as ruler of the Highlands and did not recognise some King in Edinburgh.

At this time if a Highlander felt he had been wrongly treated he went to his own chief. If he thought he still had not received fair treatment then he might go to the Lord of the Isles for justice. If he did so then it was probably at great risk to himself for Highland chiefs did not like to share their power with anyone else, including the mighty Lord of the Isles with his castle on Islay. When James IV became King the Lord of the Isles was John, chief of Clan Donald, which a Highland poet described as:

> The noblest race of all created, a race kindly, mighty, valorous [brave]: a race hottest in time of battle . . . a race without arrogance, without injustice, who seized nothing except spoils of war.

In 1493 James ordered John to give up his titles and land to the Crown. John obeyed meekly enough but his followers were not so easily overruled and made ready for war. In the years that followed James had to lead several campaigns against Clan Donald and its supporters, using his navy and cannons. Most of the chiefs in the end promised to obey James's laws but they still went on quarrelling among themselves. By 1500 James wanted to attend to other matters and so he made the Campbell Earl of Argyll his Lieutenant or Overseer in the lands he had taken from Clan Donald. A year later he put the Gordon Earls of

Huntly in charge of royal affairs in the north-east of Scotland.

Some historians say that James failed in his efforts to bring the Highlanders under his rule. They claim he had made the power of the King weaker by making the Campbells and Gordons so powerful and that these two great families often stirred up trouble for their own gain.

The Borders

James also had much trouble keeping law and order in the Borders. The Border country between Scotland and England was the home of fierce, bold cattle 'reivers' or rustlers like the Armstrongs, Maxwells and Homes who fought as bitterly among themselves as they fought the English Border families.

'Jeddart Justice'

In the past other rulers had their royal judges to enforce their laws in the Borders. James IV did not think these judges were strong enough on their own to ensure the Borderers obeyed his laws. He led several raids himself to round up law-breakers and once he brought a party of outlaws to Jedburgh with nooses already around their necks. This became known as 'Jeddart Justice'; when a man was hanged first and then sentenced! The Borderers became used to the sight of James sitting as judge in his own courts and they came to respect a King who carried out his own laws. All Scots soon came to realise that James would spare no law-breaker, no matter how powerful or rich he was.

Notice the different ways by which James brought the Borderers and Highlanders under control. Think why he had to use different methods.

The First Scottish Education Act

James was determined to have enough men who would be able to understand his laws and act as judges in local courts. And so, in 1496, the Scottish Parliament passed the first Scottish Education Act. The act said that all barons and rich landowners must send their eldest sons to school when they were eight or nine and they were to remain there until:

> Thai be copetentlie foundid [taught] and have perfite latyne, and thereftir to remane thre yeris at the sculis of art and Jure [Law]. Throw the Quilkis [which] Justice may reigne universalie throw all the realme.

(Try saying this first before you begin to translate it!)

Remember in those days Latin was the language of the law-courts. You can see that James thought that education should have a practical purpose.

Aberdeen University

In 1495, the wise Bishop of Aberdeen, William Elphinstone, founded a university there. The new university was set up for that part of the kingdom which was:

> Separated from the rest . . . by arms of the sea and very high mountains, in which dwell men rude and ignorant of letters, and almost barbarous.

This does not mean that the people of the north-east were impertinent savages but that they were thought backward. It gives us some idea of how words can change their meaning in five hundred years.

Aberdeen was the first university in Scotland to have a separate school of medicine. The new university shows us clearly how the ideas of the Renaissance were spreading, for medicine was not taught separately in the other two Scottish universities of St Andrews founded in 1411 and Glasgow founded in 1451. The Scots could now boast that they had three universities to England's two at Oxford and Cambridge!

Barbers and Surgeons

James encouraged the teaching of medicine at Aberdeen because he was interested in the subject himself. He later granted the barbers and surgeons of Edinburgh the right to form a 'gild' or society in 1505. The gild was to be given the corpse of a hanged criminal once a year on which to practise anatomy.

A sixteenth–century surgeon at work

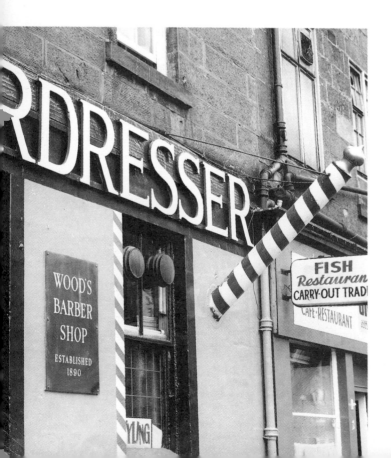

James also helped the gild's finances by giving it the sole right to sell whisky in the city! You may be surprised to find the barbers and surgeons in the same gild. At one time both barbers and surgeons practised medicine. The main treatment was by 'bleeding' the patient by opening a vein or using a leech to suck his blood. A 'leech' was the old name for a doctor. Some barbers today still have outside their shops a pole with red and white stripes on the end of which is a gold painted cup. The stripes represent the bandages and the cup was for catching the patient's blood.

A Printing Press

James also gave permission to Walter Chapman and Andrew Myllar to set up the first printing press in Scotland in 1507. The invention of the printing press meant that books could be made cheaper and more people would be able to read about the new ideas and discoveries. Although Chapman and Myllar printed the Acts of the Scottish Parliament and books by

Andrew Myllar's sign

Scottish Churchmen, they made more money by publishing tales of valiant knights rescuing maidens in distress.

Scottish Poets

Some of the most popular publications of Chapman and Myllar were books of poetry by William Dunbar and Robert Henryson. Both these poets wrote in the Lallans or Scots language that de Ayala mentioned. Both poets admired the poetry of Chaucer who wrote in English and not Latin.

William Dunbar was probably the finest poet of his times. He was a priest, a wandering beggar, and a courtier as well as a poet. Much of his poetry is about himself and his view of life. In one poem he complains to James IV that he is being neglected:

Nane can remeid my maladie [cure my sickness]
Sa weill as ye, Sir, veralie [truly]
With ane benefice [church living] ye may preiff [reprieve]
Exces of thocht [worry] lat [giving] me mischief.

He was proud of his poetry. Like many other Scottish poets he can be gloomy, but not for long. In one of his great poems, 'Lament for the Makaris [Poets]' he writes:

The stait of man dois change and varie—
Now sound, now seik, now blith now sary
Now dans and mery, now like to dee
Timor mortis conturbat me.

Translated into modern English this might be:

The life of man changes and varies
Sometimes joyful then full of worries
Merry dancing or in sickness lying
I am full of the fear of dying.

Ships and Seamen

As you have already seen, one of James's interests was a Royal Scottish Navy. By 1513 James had a fleet of twenty-four ships, most of which he bought from other countries. His pride was the *Great Michael* which was completed about 1511. It was said to be the biggest ship in all Europe, nearly 88 metres long and over 13 metres inside the hull. Its sides were nearly 3.5 metres thick. To test its strength James had a cannon fired at its side and the mighty vessel showed no damage. People marvelled at its size and it was said that all the woods in Fife had been cut down to make it. Certainly it was so huge that James had to construct a new port to build it at Newhaven.

The *Great Michael*

But ships are no good without sailors like the Barton brothers of Leith and Sir Andrew Wood of Largo who were James's favourite sailors. Sometimes however they turned their hands to piracy and this led to trouble with neighbouring countries—especially England.

The Great Crusade

With ships such as the *Great Michael* James hoped to impress other countries. Perhaps he also hoped to engage Scots in the voyages of exploration. He certainly needed a navy to protect Scottish shipping from the pirates who infested the North Sea. He would also need a navy if he wanted to carry out his dream of a great crusade against the Turks. He dreamt of uniting all the Christian rulers under his leadership which would sweep the Turks from the Holy Land. In the meantime he needed his navy to protect Scotland from the old enemy south of the Border.

The English Connection

In 1485, three years before James IV came to the throne, Henry Tudor became King of England when he defeated Richard III at Bosworth. James and Henry VII did not get on well at first but in 1503 the two Kings became friends when James married Henry's daughter, Margaret.

Henry gave James £40 000 as Margaret's dowry, or wedding settlement. This was a great deal of money for the King of a poor country like Scotland. There was a great deal of rejoicing at this 'Marriage of the Thistle and the Rose'. Expensive and elaborate preparations were made for the marriage of James and his fourteen-year-old bride. Despite all the magnificence, some of the English guests were disappointed and:

> Returned into theyre countrey, gevynge more prayse to the manhoode, than to the good manner and nurture [upbringing] of Scotland.

Battle of Flodden Field

James IV and Henry VIII

When Henry VII died in 1509 he was succeeded by his young and ambitious son, Henry VIII. In 1512 Henry was at war with Louis XII of France. Louis persuaded James to invade England in order to draw the English King's attention from France, and James agreed. On 22 August 1513 a great Scottish army marched over the Border. With it went many great cannons each dragged by twenty-two oxen. The Scots moved slowly for they did not want to venture too far into English territory. Norham Castle and a few small English forts were captured. Meanwhile an

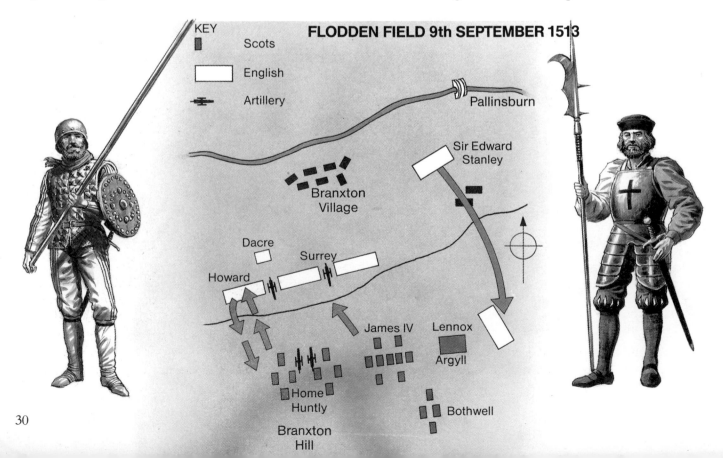

KEY
Scots
English
Artillery

FLODDEN FIELD 9th SEPTEMBER 1513

Pallinsburn

Sir Edward Stanley

Branxton Village

Dacre
Surrey
Howard

James IV
Lennox
Argyll

Home
Huntly

Bothwell

Branxton Hill

English army under the command of the seventy-year-old Earl of Surrey marched quickly north to meet the Scots. Surrey may have been old but he was a skilled and energetic general. He had many worries for supplies were running short and there was much grumbling among the English soldiers because the supply of beer had run out. When the Scots learnt of the English advance they took up a strong position on Flodden Hill overlooking the River Till.

You will see from the map on the page opposite how well the Scots had chosen their position. Surrey realised that unless he could make the Scots give up their position he would be defeated. He therefore marched his army in driving rain along the east bank of the Till which crossed by the bridge at Twizel. In this way he put the English army between the Scots and Scotland and cut off their retreat.

Surrey now turned his army south hoping to seize Branxton Hill. If he managed to do this the Scots would then have to attack the strong English position between them and their homeland. Seeing this, James quickly moved his army to occupy Branxton Hill before the English did. The Scots won the race and waited in battle-order for the English.

The Scots

If you look at the plan of the battle you will see that the Scots were arranged in five groups, very like Bruce's formations at Bannockburn. James's group which was well-equipped, was second from the right of the army. On the King's right were the Highlanders under the Earls of Argyll and Lennox. To the left of James was another division under the Earls of Crawford, Montrose and Errol. On the extreme left was another group, mostly Borderers commanded by Home and Huntly. There was a reserve behind the King's division under the Earl of Bothwell. In this order the Scots waited for the English army still struggling its way across the marshy ground at the foot of the hill.

The English

The English army was divided into a vanguard at the front commanded by Admiral Howard, Surrey's son. At the rear was Surrey who commanded the larger part of the army. Both parts had a centre and two wings.

Weapons

On that September day both armies numbered about 20 000 men. The Scottish foot soldiers had swords but their main weapon was a 5-metre long spear. The Scots' cavalry was mostly Borderers on the left wing. The Scottish cannon was good but heavy, designed more for siege warfare than for battles. Most of the English soldiers were infantrymen armed with 'halberds' or 'bills' which were shaped like a spear about 2.5 metres long but with an axe-head which could be used for cutting or slashing. The English had about 500 hundred horsemen under Lord Dacre. The English cannons were lighter than those of the Scots and were manned by German gunners who were experts at their job, unlike many Scots.

The Battle Begins

The first man on the English side to receive a shock was Admiral Howard. He had pushed his troops forward, blinded by rain and smoke from the fires the Scots had lit on Flodden. In his eagerness to seize Branxton Hill his troops had left the rest of the English army behind. Howard's shock turned to fear when the rain and smoke cleared and he saw the enemy's army looming above him. He saw the Scottish battle-formations with the watery sunshine glittering on the points of thousands of spears. Between the massed Scottish groups Howard could also see the Scottish gunners preparing to fire. Howard realised that if the Scots charged now he and his soldiers would be crushed. He tore off his neck medallion and sent a messenger to his father urging him to come to his help.

When Surrey received his son's message he urged his troops on faster than ever. Then he heard the Scots's cannons thundering.

But when Surrey reached the battle-front he felt he had been granted two miracles. The Scots had not moved. They stood still waiting for the English. The second miracle was the sound of the Scottish cannon balls growling *over* the heads of the English troops. The inexperienced Scottish gunners had been unable to lower their guns enough to fire into the English troops.

Surrey gave orders to his German gunners to open fire and the English shot began to tear gaps in the Scots' ranks. One by one the Scottish guns were silenced by this deadly fire. On the Scots' left, Huntly and Home whose troops had suffered most from the English guns, ordered their men to charge. The Borderers swept down and tore through Howard's troops, many of whom began to flee. Seeing this, Dacre moved his horsemen into the battle to stop the

Scots. Then followed a confused, bitter fight—but the Scots were stopped.

James Moves

When James saw the effects of the Borderers' charge he thought his moment of victory had come. He had sent his own war-horse to the rear for he wanted to fight on foot at the head of his men. He ordered his division to advance and it must have struck a chill in many English hearts when they saw the great steel wave bearing down on them. The Scots reached the bottom of the hill, scattering any resistance. Then they found themselves trying to charge 180 metres uphill to get at the main body of Surrey's army. The ground had become so slippery with blood and rain that many Scots took off their boots to get a better grip. They fought their way grimly up the hill. Both sides fought in silence, saving their breath for the grim business of killing. In the hand-to-hand fighting the Scots found their spears useless against the English 'bills' which chopped off the spear-points. Many of the Scots, including their King, flung away their useless spears and settled down to sword-work. But these were no match for the longer bills with their biting axe-heads. James fought his way ahead, killing as he went, until he was within a spear's length of Surrey. Then his sword was knocked from his hand and he was hurled to the ground where he was trapped in his heavy armour. As he lay helpless he saw the axe-heads being raised to kill. . .

Battle's End

On another part of the field the Highlanders stood watching the bloody struggle before them. Under the cover of the rain Sir Edward Stanley with about 5000 men from Cheshire and Lancashire crept behind and to the right of the Highlanders. Stanley ordered his bowmen to shoot and then charged, driving the Highlanders into Bothwell's reserves. Instead of fighting, some of the Scots began to plunder their own dead until the English cut them down. Many Scots began to flee and when Stanley's men charged the King's division in the rear the battle was decided.

The struggle did not end then for many of the Scots fought dourly and died around their King's body. Only when night fell did they finally give up, breaking into small groups to try and escape to Scotland.

Twelve thousands Scots died on Flodden Field. Their bodies were buried in great pits where a monument to the dead now stands. Among these dead were the King and his illegitimate son, the Archbishop of St Andrews. With them died two bishops, three abbots, nine earls, fourteen lords and three Highland chiefs. As the old song put it, 'the Flowers of the forest were we'ed awa'.

Aftermath

King James's body was never recovered by the Scots. Soon rumours began to circulate that he had escaped from the battlefield and had finally gone on a pilgrimage to Jerusalem. Lord Dacre said that the Scots:

> Love me worst of any Englisheman living, be reason that I fande [found] the body of the King of Scotts, slayne in the felde.

We know so much about the details of the battle from accounts written about it afterwards. Only one of these was written by a Scot but several were written by Englishmen. The Scots wanted no remembrance of Flodden Field.

Something to Remember

Flodden marks the end to all the hopes that James's reign had brought about. The idea of a Great Crusade died with James. The pride of his navy, the *Great Michael* was sold and ended up a rotten hulk in a French harbour without having fired a shot in anger. James had tried to unite the country and ensure that his laws were obeyed. Most of his successes were undone by his early death. He tried to make Scotland respected among the other European states: defeat at Flodden only showed up Scotland's weaknesses.

Something to Think About

James's successor was an infant and the country was plunged into a number of warring groups each trying to gain power. This undid much of James's work. Some historians have said that James's ambitions outstripped both his own and his country's means and that Scotland could never have been more than a second-rate power. Again it has been said that James failed to bring the Highlanders under his rule. In fact by handing so much power over to his lieutenants he really weakened royal power in those parts.

Perhaps the many advances which occurred during his reign would have happened anyway and James has received undue credit in this way. In the same way, many 'great' men have received the credit for other people's achievements.

A Revolution in Religion [3]

The Beggars' Summons

Early on New Year's Day 1559 those people who had got up early were surprised to see a notice posted on the doors of buildings where the friars lived. These notices went up on friary doors in many Scottish towns. Those who could read saw that the notice had been signed by:

> The Blynd, Cruked [Lame], Bedrelles [Bed-ridden] and all other Pure [Poor] sa viseit be [afflicted by] the hand of God, as may not work.

This 'Beggars' Summons' ordered the friars to leave their friaries by Whitsun (May) 1559 and give them to the poor people. It was written by those who were protesting against the life that many bishops, priests, monks and friars were leading. These protestors or Protestants wanted Catholic churchmen to change their way of life.

Many sincere Catholics were also displeased with the behaviour of many Catholic churchmen. A Church rule said that churchmen could not marry but both Catholics and Reformers pointed out bishops and priests who lived with women by whom they had children. Many knew that John Hamilton, Archbishop of St Andrews, the highest churchman in all Scotland, had seven illegitimate children.

Reformers made fun of parish priests who could barely read and write and who knew no Latin, the language of Catholic services. Good Catholics were also ashamed of priests who: 'stammer and stumble in mid-course of reading'. Many of these chaplains were so poor that they tried to get more money by trading and so neglected their church duties. This became so bad that a church law was passed which said:

> ... that no cleric [churchman] having the means of an honourable livelihood according to his own calling, engage in secular [non-religious] pursuits, especially by trading.

Other clerics would demand presents before they would conduct funeral or baptism services.

In a play of the time called *The Thrie Estaites* written by Sir Robert Lindsay of the Mount, much scorn is poured on the lives of churchmen. In one part Lindsay tells what happened to a poor man when his mother and father died. The local laird and priest took his horse and two cows. The man's wife died and the priest took another cow and his best clothes, so that:

> Quhen [When] all was gane, I micht mak na debate [had no choice]
> Bot with my bairns past for till [to] beg my meat...

The Wealth of the Church

Historians have worked out that the Catholic Church owned from one-third to one-half of the land of Scotland. Its yearly income was about £300 000 (Scots) when that of the Crown was only £17 000 (Scots). Though the Church was very wealthy bishops and other high-ranking churchmen took much for themselves and left very little for the poor parish priests.

Pluralists
An abbot or a bishop might receive money for being the chaplain to several village churches. Such a person would be called a 'pluralist' because he had more than one church living. He would pay a small sum of money to a 'vicar' to take his place and naturally the vicar usually neglected such a poorly paid living.

Greedy Kings and Nobles
Much of the Catholic Church's wealth also went into the pockets of the King and the nobles. Alexander Stewart, the Archbishop of St Andrews, who was killed at Flodden, was an illegitimate son of James IV. James had made him Archbishop when Alexander was only eleven but James used the Archbishop's income as though it belonged to him. Four of James V's illegitimate sons became Abbots of Melrose, Kelso, Holyrood and Coldingham. The nobles were quick to follow the royal example and many took over Church property and used it as though it were their own.

Commendators

Sometimes these royal or noble sons never took the holy orders that would allow them to perform church services. They were the heads of abbeys but were called 'commendators' and not abbots. One of these commendators was Mark Kerr of Cessford who was Commendator of Newbattle Abbey while James Haswell was Abbot. These commendators tried to get as much money as they could from the abbeys' lands even though they neglected the monks and the abbey buildings.

The Church Tries to Reform Itself

Many sincere Catholics wanted to stop all these people from using the Church for their own profit. Between 1549 and 1559 they held three Councils to reform the Church. These Councils passed laws to stop priests living with women and buying and selling goods.

The Councils also wanted priests to be properly educated. Archbishop Hamilton ordered a book called the *Catechism* to be written in English so that the people could understand the questions in it and the replies they had to make. The Councils even said that priests were not to grow beards and were to dress in a sober and dignified manner. In the end these reforms failed because many of the people who were supposed to see that the new rules were obeyed, did not want the Church to be reformed.

Protesting Heretics

While some men were trying to carry out the Councils' reforms many others were adopting the ideas of the Protestant Reformers. On the Continent people had begun to criticise the Catholic Church at the beginning of the sixteenth century. In 1517 a German friar called Martin Luther spoke out against the payment of money for the forgiving of sins.

Many listened to his protest and joined in Luther's attempts to reform the Church. Gradually, these Reformers wanted greater changes. They wanted to do away with the power of the Pope in the Church. They also believed that the Bible should be the only source of belief for Christians, for they said that the Bible was God's Word and no man could change it.

The Reek of Master Hamilton

Followers of Luther's ideas came to Scotland and preached them. This was a dangerous thing to do for they went against the teachings of the Catholic Church which regarded the Reformers as 'heretics' or unbelievers. One of these Reformers or heretics, depending on which side you were on, was Patrick Hamilton who had been Abbot of Fearn in Easter Ross. He was burnt at the stake on the orders of Archbishop Beaton in 1528 for spreading Luther's teachings. At the burning one of Beaton's friends turned to him and said:

> My Lord, if you burn any more let them be burned in deep cellars; for the reek [smoke] of Master Hamilton has infected as many as it blew upon.

Think what the speaker meant when he said the 'reek' would infect people.

For a few years after this the Protestant Reformers were quiet though many more people began to accept their beliefs.

Henry VIII's Church Reforms

What stopped many Scots from becoming Protestants was that Henry VIII of England had replaced the Pope by himself as the Head of the Anglican (English) Church. Many Scots therefore thought that Protestants supported the English King. Henry tried to persuade his nephew, James V of Scotland, to do the same as he had done but James refused. After all, James V was able to extract a great deal of money from the Catholic Church without the need for reform.

The nephew of Archbishop Beaton, David Beaton, was made a Cardinal in 1538 and succeeded his uncle as Archbishop in 1539. Of Cardinal Beaton it has been said:

> His high station [position] in the Church placed him in the way of great employments [important work]; his abilities were equal to the greatest of these, nor did he reckon any of them to be above his merit... He was one of the worst of men—a proud, cruel, unrelenting and licentious [loose-living] tyrant.

This was the most powerful churchman in Scotland.

George Wishart

Beaton persecuted Protestants because he regarded them as heretics and, he said, because they supported Henry VIII. His chief victim was George Wishart who had been a pupil and master at Montrose Grammar School. On 1 March 1546 Wishart was burnt at St Andrews for spreading false beliefs. He was accused of spreading the heretical ideas which he

James V

Mary of Guise

'Wishart's Last Prayer'

had learnt from John Calvin, a Frenchman who had settled in Geneva in Switzerland.

John Calvin
Calvin was even more critical of the Catholic Church than Luther had been. He wanted many more changes. He wanted to get rid of all bishops as well as the Pope. Under Calvin's system the congregation of each church ran its own affairs. Each congregation would choose elders and deacons who would help run the church. Each congregation would also choose its own minister or preacher of sermons who would also lead the services. All the congregations in a district would send representatives to local assemblies called 'presbyteries' and so Calvin's followers were sometimes called Presbyterians. Presbyterians did not say mass and no prayers were offered to the Virgin Mary or the saints. Presbyterians regarded this as idol-worshipping and did not approve of statues in their churches.

John Knox
In Scotland the man most responsible for spreading Calvin's ideas was John Knox. He was born in Haddington and probably went to the grammar school there. We know little about his early life but by 1546 he had given up the priesthood and become a follower of Wishart. On the night that Wishart was taken prisoner Knox wanted to go with him but, sensing what was to happen, Wishart turned to Knox and said:

> Nay, return to your bairns [pupils] and God bless you, one is enough for the sacrifice...

The Assassination of Beaton
On Saturday 29 May 1546 the inhabitants of St Andrews were aroused by the church bells sounding the alarm. When they arrived at the gates of the Castle they saw the dead body of Cardinal Beaton hanging over the walls by a hand and a foot. His assassins had seized the Castle and Knox joined them there

HOW PRESBYTERIANS RAN THEIR CHURCHES

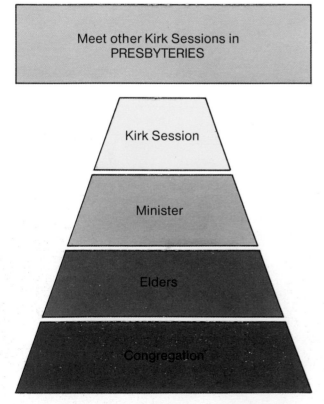

John Knox

to act as their minister. Very soon a French force besieged the Castle and after a bitter struggle the defenders were forced to surrender.

The Galley Slave

Though his life was spared Knox was sentenced to the living death of a galley slave. Later, he wrote a book called *Historie of the Reformatioun of Religion within the Realm of Scotland* which told how the Scottish prisoners tied up their French guards when they were drunk and so made their escape, although: 'Great search was made through the whole country for them.'

Some historians say that Knox was released at the request of Edward VI, the new King of England, who had succeeded his father Henry VIII. We know that Knox was a free man in England by 1549. He soon drew attention to himself by his powerful preaching in Berwick, Newcastle and London. Edward VI offered him a bishopric but he refused. Knox knew that Edward VI was unwell and that when he died he would be succeeded by his sister, Mary Tudor, who was a staunch Catholic.

The English Take a Hand

Mary Tudor

When she became Queen, Mary set out to undo all the religious changes that her father and brother had made. She had many English Protestants burnt, but Knox escaped to the Continent and went to Geneva where he became an enthusiastic supporter of Calvin. In 1558 Mary Tudor died and was succeeded by her sister, Elizabeth I, who followed her father's policies.

Elizabeth and the Regent Mary

It now looked as if the great Catholic powers of France and Spain might join in a Crusade against Elizabeth's England. In Scotland the young Catholic Queen Mary had been sent to France for safety and the government was in the hands of Queen Mary's mother, the Regent Mary of Guise. The Catholic Regent thought that the Scottish Reformers would try to gain the support of Elizabeth to stop the French using Scotland as a 'back door' to attack England. Mary of Guise asked the French for help and French troops were sent to Leith to check the Scottish Reformers.

A view of Perth, *c.* 1700

The Lords of the Congregation

Many Protestant nobles and lairds watched the growing power of the Regent with alarm. They decided to band themselves into an army and declared:

> We shall maintain them, nourish them and defend them, the whole congregation of CHRIST, and every member [person] thereof, by our whole power, and spend our lives against Satan and all wicked power that do intend tyranny and trouble against the foresaid congregation.

Reformers and Revolutionaries

These 'Lords of the Congregation' as they were called could call upon many followers to support their cause. They gave the Reformers the armed power they would need in the coming struggle against the Regent.

The Lords asked Knox to return to Scotland and preach to the people. On 11 May 1559 he preached to the people of Perth. The sermon sparked off a riot in which church buildings were destroyed and looted. A civil war had begun.

The Siege of Leith

The Regent's troops retired to Leith where they waited on French supplies and reinforcements. All the Reformers' attempts to capture Leith failed for

The Siege of Leith, 1560 from a sixteenth-century print

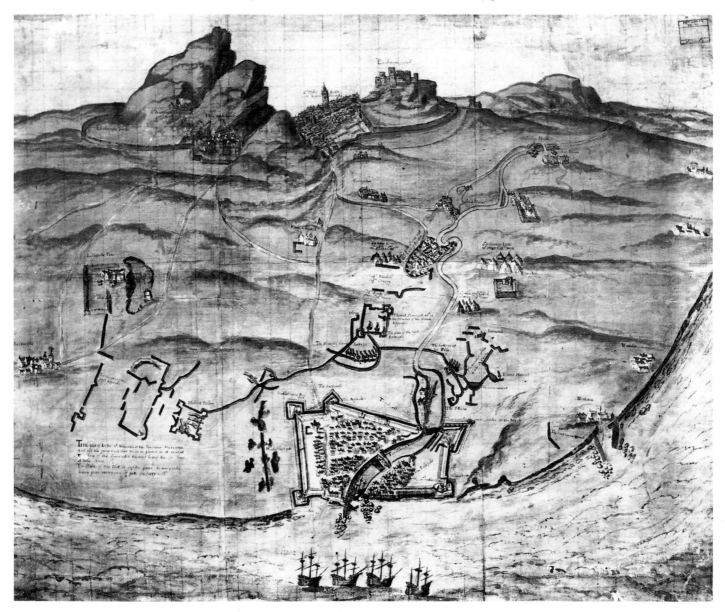

they did not have powerful enough cannons to destroy the walls of the fortress. The only military aid the Reformers could get was from Elizabeth who listened to their pleas for help. Elizabeth did not like subjects who rebelled against their rulers for that might encourage some English people to do the same. She particularly disliked Knox for he had written a pamphlet against *all* women rulers. However, she knew she had to help the Scottish Reformers before the French could land troops and so she sent an English fleet to the Forth to stop any French ships. Shortly afterwards she sent an English army and artillery which forced the French garrison to surrender. The Regent died in Edinburgh Castle on 11 June 1560 and less than a month later the Treaty of Edinburgh was signed between the French and English.

The treaty said:

> ... that all military forces, land and naval, of each party shall withdraw from the realm of Scotland.

With the Regent dead, the French out of the way and Queen Mary still in France, the Reformers could now carry out their plans of replacing the Catholic Church with their Reformed Kirk.

The Reformed Kirk

The First Book of Discipline

In May 1560 the Reformers produced their first set of rules for the new Kirk. This was the *First Book of Discipline*. These rules were not just for the new Kirk, they were to change the lives of the Scottish people as well. The *Book* said that all monasteries, friaries, nunneries and chapels were to be closed down. Each Kirk was to choose its own minister who was to be ordained, or passed, by a bishop or superintendant. The title of superintendant was a new one made by the Kirk to take the place of a bishop who had remained Catholic. The ministers were to preach sermons every day and people were to attend Kirk every Sunday. A Bible written in English was to be kept in each Kirk for every one to read.

A School in Every Parish

The Reformers wanted a school set up in every parish and town. In each parish there was to be a special house where poor people could be looked after. The Reformers wanted people educated enough for everyone to be able to read the Bible.

The New Ministers

The Reformers would have liked to provide a minister for each congregation but there were few men sufficiently trained for this. Some men who had been priests and monks joined the Kirk and devoted their lives to their new congregations. The success of the new Kirk owed much to these men.

In December 1560 some ministers and 'notable nobles and barons professing [following] the true religion' as well as representatives from the burghs met in the first General Assembly of the Reformed Kirk. These general assemblies were rather like Church parliaments which met to decide the Kirk's business. They were to have an important say in the way the Kirk was organised.

Money

The money for all these schemes was supposed to come from the wealth of the Catholic Church. Here the Reformers ran into difficulties. As you have seen, much of the wealth of the Old Church had been taken over by the Crown and nobles and they were unwilling to part with it. In the end only one-third of the Old Church's wealth was given to the new Kirk. As well as this the salaries of Catholic churchmen who had become Protestants was paid until they died. John Knox summed up this settlement in his usual blunt fashion:

> I see two parts given to the Devil, and the third part must be divided between God and the Devil.

Presbyterians

Twenty years after this, in the 1580s, a group of men began to seek changes in the organisation of the Kirk. They wanted it to be more like the Presbyterian system of John Calvin. They wanted rid of all bishops and wanted ministers and elders to meet in presbyteries. The presbyteries would choose and ordain new ministers for their district. The 'Presbyterians' now wanted all the wealth of the Old Church given to the Kirk. All ministers would be equal in rank; they would have 'parity' as it was called. They also wanted yearly meetings of the General Assembly. This, as you can see, would not be liked by the Crown and many nobles who thought that the Kirk and its ministers was becoming too powerful. This was to cause much trouble in the future.

Something to Remember

The Reformation in religion began because some people thought there were many things wrong in the Catholic Church. They said that many churchmen were living lives unfitting for those who had taken Holy Orders. As the Reformers believed that only the Bible was the word of God, they said that only those beliefs found in the Bible were the correct ones. This led them to reject those beliefs which had grown up in the Catholic Church over fifteen centuries. What the Reformers wanted to do was to change the Church back to what it had been in the times of Jesus and His Apostles.

Many sincere Catholics also wanted to reform their Church but, unfortunately, there were too many men who were interested only in its power and wealth. Before the Catholic reformers could make any changes they found it was too late for Protestant Reformers such as Luther and Calvin wanted nothing to do with the Catholic Church.

In Scotland the Protestants found that they had to fight the Crown as well as the Catholics because Scottish kings had used much of the wealth of the Catholic Church for their own purposes. This meant that the Reformers had to carry out a *political* revolution as well as a *religious* one. As the Crown had the help of the French, the Reformers sought English aid in their struggle. When the Reformers won their battle against the Regent Mary they began to carry out their religious revolution.

Something to Think About

Some historians have blamed Knox and the other Reformers for making the Scottish peoples' lives dull and gloomy because they made very strict rules about how people should live their lives. But we must remember that they were very sincere and wanted to make people live according to the Good Book. Certainly some of Knox's followers often interfered in peoples' lives too much, but even Catholic Churchmen have praised Knox for his sincerity though they disagreed with his views. Knox was not always the kill-joy he has been made out to be. He once told Mary Queen of Scots that he quite approved of dancing!

The Reformers have also been blamed for the destruction of many beautiful old church buildings. It is true that many statues and other decorations were destroyed at the time of the Reformation. Remember the mob in Perth. Knox was disgusted at their behaviour and called them a 'rascally multitude' for he wanted to preserve church buildings for the new Kirk as much as he wanted rid of friars and monks. Much greater damage was done to church buildings by years of neglect before and after the Reformation. In the Borders most of the abbeys were destroyed by the armies of Henry VIII which invaded Scotland in 1544 and 1547.

For all its narrow-mindedness the Reformed Kirk made great changes in the lives of the Scottish people. The need to read the Bible produced a people who were able to read—and often think—for themselves. It also helped people to become independent and critical. If it had done nothing else then the Reformation would still have been one of the greatest events in the history of the Scottish people.

The Wisest Fool in Christendom

One Man; Two Views

In his [James VI's] dealings alike with Highland chiefs and Presbyterian clergy he so often displayed a petty malice [spite], a malignity [viciousness] and a deliberate cruelty, that we are bound to conclude that those vices were of the essence [heart and soul] of his nature.

> (P. Hume Brown, *History of Scotland* Vol. II, 1911)

James [VI] . . . had some admirable traits [qualities of character]. He was warm-hearted, affectionate and generous, and had a genuine love of peace and dislike of violence . . .

> (Alan G. R. Smith, *The Reign of James VI and I*, Problems in Focus, Macmillan 1973)

The young James VI

Both these descriptions were written by historians. But look at *when* each was written. Sometimes two people can come to very different conclusions about the same person.

The Young King

On 24 July 1567 James VI was crowned King of the Scots. He was only one year old. Stranger still, he was crowned King while his mother, Mary Queen of Scots, was still alive. She had been forced to flee for safety to England by a rebellion of Scottish nobles and Protestant ministers. Mary remained a prisoner in England until her execution in 1567. 1587

The young King was an orphan because his father, Lord Darnley, had been murdered some years before. James grew up a lonely child, deprived of the love of his father and mother. His life was not made any easier by his chief teacher, George Buchanan. Buchanan was a true 'Renaissance' man famed throughout Europe for his learning. It was said that Buchanan could write better Latin than the Roman writer Cicero!

The Execution of Mary, Queen of Scots

Buchanan was a great scholar but he was harsh and bad-tempered towards his royal pupil. Above all, Buchanan hated Mary Stuart and did his best to turn James against his mother.

James, however, was a very clever pupil and Buchanan gave him an excellent, if strict, education. James's schoolday began very early for he said long prayers and had his Greek lessons *before* breakfast. Afterwards, there was Latin until dinner-time which was followed by Essay-writing, Arithmetic, Geography and Astronomy. Before his lessons finished for the day James also learnt some History and French. Then, at last, James was allowed to pursue his favourite sport of hunting. By the time he was eight, James could translate aloud in French from a Latin Bible and then translate the French into English. At fifteen he was said to be the best educated monarch in all Christendom.

Was James a Coward?

As James grew up people noticed his fear of violence. Some said he was a coward. The Englishman Sir John Oglander wrote:

King James was the most cowardly man that I ever knew. He could not endure a soldier; to hear of war was death to him and how he tormented himself with fear of some sudden mischief [attack] may be proved by his great quilted doublets [jackets], pistol-proof.

However, when we remember that James's father had been murdered and his mother's life had been threatened just before James was born, we can perhaps understand why James had good reasons for fearing assassination. There were also several attempts to kidnap the young King, some of them successful. James spent long periods of his childhood in the hands of some of the gangsters who called themselves Scottish noblemen. Try to imagine how you would feel if all these violent things had happened to you. Two years after he became King of England in 1603 James was threatened by a plot to blow him up, in the same way as his father had been murdered. This was the famous 'Gunpowder Plot' of Guy Fawkes in 1605. So it looks as though James lived in constant fear for his life.

The Gunpowder Plot, 1605. The scene on the right shows what was supposed to happen

Was James a Liar?

A historian, writing about 1900, called James a 'dissembler', that is a person who disguises his or her true feelings. Perhaps he learned to be a dissembler when he was in the hands of his kidnappers. He pretended to like them and do what they wanted when he really hated them. Here is a poem he wrote when he was fifteen:

> Thought unreveeled can doe no ill,
> But words past out turn not again [But spoken
>   words cannot be changed]
> Be careful, ay [always] for to invent [devise]
> The way to gett thyne own intent [desires].

These few lines of poetry tell us a great deal about James's character. Here he is speaking openly and not trying to conceal anything. If you look carefully at the picture of James on page 44 painted in later life you can still see a certain wariness in his eyes.

The Wisest Fool in Christendom

Because he was clever James liked to show off his learning. Perhaps he did this too often for one of his courtiers called him a fool—though not when James could hear him! When another courtier heard this he said that if James was a fool then he was the Wisest Fool in Christendom.

Royal Dislikes

James tended to make up his mind quickly about things and stick to his ideas. He hated tobacco-smoking and even wrote a book about the evils of smoking. He was fascinated by witchcraft for, like most people of his time, he firmly believed that witches had the power to do evil. He used his power to personally persecute those whom he thought were guilty of witchcraft. He was responsible for the torture and burning of many men and women accused of witchcraft.

King and Kirk

You probably remember those Presbyterians who after 1580 wanted a stricter system of governing the Church. They also said that the King should rule Scotland for God. This was their way of saying that the King should do as they told him. At the same time these Presbyterians thought that the King should just be an ordinary member of the Kirk, like everyone else. James thought differently. As far as he was concerned, James believed that God had chosen him to be King and that he was responsible to God alone. He was determined to rule Scotland in his way and stop any threat to his power. One of the biggest threats was the Kirk, which he wanted to bring under royal control. Since he could appoint bishops he brought them back into the Kirk as a means of controlling it.

James and the Highlands

Another threat to his power were the Highlanders. Like most of his Lowland subjects James disliked the Highlanders. He showed no mercy in stamping out clan feuds. At one time the Clan MacGregor caused him so much trouble that he outlawed the whole clan and ordered that no one was to have the name Mac-Gregor!

King and Nobles

Many of James's ancestors had been threatened by rebellious nobles. Some had even been murdered by them. His own life had been at risk several times from their plots. He hated the feuds they fought among themselves and forbade them to carry weapons in his presence. Though he punished those who rebelled against him he more often gained their loyalty by friendship. James needed men whom he could trust and he began to rely on the sons of the lesser nobility and the country lairds. This was unlike previous kings who had chosen great noblemen for their officials. James said he preferred to have officials whom he could hang if he wanted to! When he left

Scotland in 1603 he was able to leave the government of the country in the hands of a few officials who obeyed his orders. He was so proud of his achievements in curbing the Kirk and the nobles that he once boasted that he was able to rule Scotland by the pen which his ancestors had not been able to do by the sword!

His Greatest Success

James's greatest success, his 'great prize' as he called it, was when he became King of England in 1603. For years he had tried to persuade Queen Elizabeth to chose him as her successor, but always she had refused. However, James had several important Englishmen working secretly for his cause—they had to work in secret for Elizabeth would have been extremely angry if she had known. When Elizabeth died these Englishmen sent Sir Robert Carey to tell James the news. It took Carey only three days to make the long journey on horseback from London to Edinburgh and on 24 March 1603 Carey knelt before the delighted James to tell him he was now James I, King of the United Kingdom of Scotland and England.

James as King of Scotland and England

What is Your Verdict?

So, was James a weak coward and a fool, or was he a clever and strong ruler? Perhaps he was all these things. Historians have not always agreed, as you can see if you read the two extracts on p.41 again. Early historians often accused him of being a weak and unsuccessful ruler of England. This was mainly because they believed what Englishmen said about this strange, 'foreign' King. Later historians have looked very carefully at what he actually did as King of the Scots *before* he went to England. This has made them come up with a different verdict from that of earlier, more 'English-centred' historians. From the evidence you have read you can reach your own verdict on James.

On this page and pages 46–7 you can see what a typical Scottish burgh looked like at the end of the sixteenth century. There was a high street, the main street of the town and the burgh kirk at one end. Near the kirk was the mercat or market cross from which the king's or burgh's proclamations were made. Nearby was the tron where goods were weighed. Around the mercat cross you would see the booths or stalls of the traders. There was always a great deal of activity on market days as people gossiped and argued adding to the sound of tradesmen shouting out the cheapness and quality of their wares. On fair or holy days there was great excitement as the craft gilds took part in a procession to the kirk. Each gild had its own saint and scenes were shown of how the saints had met their deaths. Sometimes to the delight of the crowd the gilds might put on a play—one of the favourites was the 'Massacre of the Innocents by Herod' which the Hammermen (smiths) of Edinburgh put on at the Feast of Corpus Christi in mid-June.

Each burgh jealously guarded its right to be the only trading centre in the locality. Each craft gild was very careful to make sure that only its members could practice that trade in the town. The craft gilds sought to punish any person carrying on a trade who was not a member of the gild.

The most powerful and wealthy of the gilds was the Merchant Gild whose members were the only ones allowed to engage in trade with foreign countries. The Merchant Gild made it almost impossible for a member of a craft gild to become a merchant. As the burgh council which governed the burgh was made up almost entirely of merchants, you can see how this made their gild even more powerful. The burghs had their own parliament called the Convention of Royal Burghs to which each burgh sent members from the burgh council. At the Conventions all matters dealing with the commercial life of the country were discussed, such as royal taxes, piracy and trade with foreign countries.

'No craftsman shall use any manner of merchandise [practise as a merchant] within the burgh but occupy his own craft, under the penalty of £10... And also that no person shall voyage to Flanders or France with merchandise, but that he is burgess or indweller within the burgh.'
(Edinburgh Council Records, 4/12/1500)

'No butcher sell any of their skins or hides that they slay nor tallow but to free merchants within the burgh.'
(Aberdeen Burgh Records, 5/4/1529)

'... the merchants of this realm, at their expense, build a ship for clearing of our Sovereign's seas of pirates and wicked persons.'
(Records of the Convention of Royal Burghs, 1/7/1574)

'William Lawsoun admitted to the gild of barbours [barbers] of Edinburgh to kow [cut hair?], schave, washe and to make whisky only. Likewise the said William Lawsoun binds [pledges] himself that he shall not practice the art of surgery...'
(Gild of Barbours of Edinburgh)

Tolboo

'Jougs'

'[Craft Gilds will] take and sufficiently take care of and prevent from begging their own poor, such as sick craftsmen, with their wives and bairns and workmen.'

(Deacons of Craft Gilds of Edinburgh, 23/3/1580)

'Because the burgh commons [land which belonged to the burgh] are rented to gentlemen who live outside the burghs . . . the magistrates of each burgh . . . shall report management, not only in the auctioning of common lands but in walking the boundaries of the burgh, once a year.'

(Convention of Royal Burghs, 13/6/1592)

'As to the size of the town [Edinburgh], it may be a mile long and half a mile wide. It has no beauty except that of its great street [the High Street] which stretches from one end of the town to the other, and is both wide and straight as well as of great length. As regards its buildings they are by no means sumptious [luxurious], since almost all are constructed of wood.'

(Henri, Duc de Rohan, 1600)

Castle

Tron

Mercat Cross

5 Royal Rights, Rebellions and Revolution

Land of Promise

On his journey from Edinburgh to London to be crowned King of England, James VI was greatly impressed by the wealth of his new kingdom. He saw the stately houses of the English nobility were like royal palaces in Scotland. He visited many of these palatial houses to indulge his passion for hunting. As he himself said:

> [I am] ... like a poor man wandering about forty years in a wilderness and barren soil and now arrived at the land of promise.

God Chooses Kings

There was much more in England which appealed to James. He believed that kings were chosen by God and as he said himself:

> The state of monarchy is the supremest thing on earth; for kings are not only God's lieutenants on earth, but even by God himself they are called gods.

This might seem like boasting to you but to James it was the plain truth. He believed that God had chosen him to rule over his Scottish and English subjects. To disobey God's chosen ruler was to disobey both God and the King.

The King as Head of the Church

The Church of England also mightily appealed to James; especially as the King was also the Head of the Anglican Church. What made it even better in his eyes was that all the parishes in England were grouped into 'dioceses' each ruled by a bishop. And, even better, the bishops were appointed by the King—himself. This was the kind of Church that James had looked forward to in his book, *Basilikon Doron*, written for his elder son, Henry, in 1598. James advised Henry what kind of churchmen to choose:

> ... advance the godly, learned men of the ministry whom of (God be praised) there lacketh not a reasonable number: and by their preferment [appointment] to bishoprics ... shall also re-establish the old institution of the three estates in parliament [bishops, lords and commons], which can no otherwise be done [cannot be done any other way].

Notice how James sees the bishops as more than just church rulers. If they were made a part of the Scottish Estates or Parliament and accepted the King as Head of the Kirk then this would strengthen the King's control over the Estates. In turn this would increase the King's power to govern the country. And here, in England, was exactly what James had always wanted in Scotland, bishops in Parliament. No wonder James was so pleased, particularly when he recalled his long struggle with the Presbyterian Kirk in Scotland.

James and the Presbyterians

The Presbyterians agreed with James that kings were chosen by God but said that kings could rule only as long as they obeyed God's word in the Bible. The Bible would be interpreted by the ministers of God—themselves. Presbyterians said that as bishops are not mentioned in the Bible they should not be allowed to exist. Though the King might have been chosen to rule by God, to the Presbyterians he was no better than anyone else in God's eyes. In a Presbyterian Church all the ministers were equal and none should be placed above the other. As you can see there was no place for bishops in their kind of church.

You can see that James would not like a church which did not give him the power and authority he wanted. In 1612, after he had seen how useful English bishops could be to him, he ordered that bishops be brought back into the Scottish Kirk. After another bitter struggle James managed to bring back holy days such as Easter and Christmas, things which the Presbyterian ministers did not like. By the Five Articles of Perth in 1618 children were to be blessed by

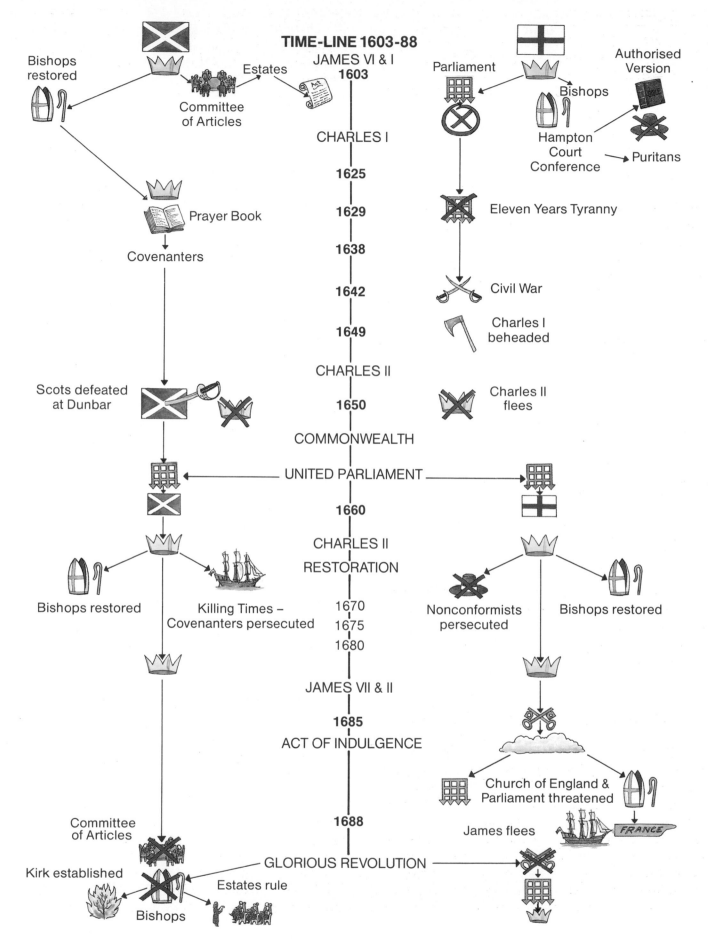

TIME-LINE 1603-88

Bishops restored

Committee of Articles

Estates

JAMES VI & I
1603

Parliament

Bishops

Authorised Version

Hampton Court Conference

Puritans

Prayer Book

Covenanters

CHARLES I

1625

1629

1638

1642

1649

Eleven Years Tyranny

Civil War

Charles I beheaded

Scots defeated at Dunbar

CHARLES II

1650

COMMONWEALTH

Charles II flees

UNITED PARLIAMENT

1660

CHARLES II RESTORATION

Bishops restored

Killing Times – Covenanters persecuted

1670

1675

1680

Nonconformists persecuted

Bishops restored

JAMES VII & II

1685

ACT OF INDULGENCE

Church of England & Parliament threatened

1688

James flees

Committee of Articles

GLORIOUS REVOLUTION

FRANCE

Kirk established

Estates rule

Bishops

49

the bishops and, during Communion services:

> . . . Be celebrate to the peoplle humblie and
> reverentlie kneeling upon their knees.

The Quarrel over Prayer Books

Kneeling during services caused a great deal of head-shaking among staunch Presbyterians because they thought this would make them like Catholics—but they accepted it, if unwillingly. The one thing they refused to accept was James's wish to use a Prayer Book during the services. Presbyterian congregations wanted their ministers to preach sermons and make up prayers on the spur of the moment. They did not want their prayers already set down in a book. James, who knew 'the stomach of that people', realised he had gone too far and introduced no more new ideas into the Presbyterian Kirk. Things settled down and it looked as though a time of peace had come to the Scottish Kirk.

James and the Puritans

There were people in England who wanted to make the services of the Anglican Church more simple. These 'Puritans', like the Presbyterians, wanted a church without bishops. They asked James to preside over a meeting between them and the bishops at Hampton Court in 1604. James was delighted to do so for he always liked showing off his knowledge of religious matters. At the beginning of the meeting he made an important statement:

> . . . he saw no cause so much to alter and change any thing, as to confirm that which he found well settled already.

In other words he saw no point in changing the Anglican Church which he regarded as perfect.

Things went quite well until the second day. A Puritan speaker, perhaps hoping to flatter James as King of the Scots, said he thought the 'presbyter' church was the ideal one. James exploded with rage and exclaimed the presbyters agreed no more with the monarchy than the Devil with God:

> Then Jack and Tom and Will and Dick shall meet, and at their pleasures censure [criticise] me and my Council and all our proceedings.

He then gave his opinion: 'No Bishop, no King; no Nobility'.

That pretty well finished the meeting. The only lasting thing to come out of the Hampton Court Conference was the Authorised Version of the Bible which was published in 1611 and which has shaped English language and literature more than any other book.

Disappointed, the Puritans turned to the English Parliament for support from the growing number of Puritans in the House of Commons. This was to be one of the greatest causes of trouble between King and Parliament in the coming years.

Kings and Parliaments:

Royal Rights

Parliament was one part of English life that James had some doubts about—especially the powers of Parliament. In this way the English Parliament was very different from the Scottish Estates. James had used the Estates like a kind of rubber-stamp to pass the laws sent to it by the Committee of the Articles which was made up of James's trusted men in Scotland. It was because of the Committee of the Articles that James made his boast of ruling Scotland by the pen. As James had written in his *Trew Law of Free Monarchies* in 1598:

> For albeit that the King make daily statutes and ordinances [laws and orders] enjoyning such pains thereto as hee thinks meet [with any penalties he thinks correct], without any advice of Parliament or Estates; yet it lies in the power of no Parliament, to make any kind of Law or Statute, without his sceptre [approval] be to it, for giving it the force of law.

The King gave his assent to any law by touching it with his sceptre. Notice what James is saying; he can make laws by his own powers or prerogative but no law can be passed by a Parliament without his consent. James is also saying that no Parliament has the right to a say in the King's affairs.

Parliament's Rights

Let us see what the English Parliament thought of James's ideas. James claimed the right to carry out relations with other countries in his way, as all previous rulers had done. In 1621 the House of Com-

The British Isles—important places in the seventeenth century

Aberdeen

Fort William

Killiecrankie

Glencoe   Dundee

Inverary   Perth

Edinburgh   **Dunbar**

Glasgow   **Rullion Green**

Bothwell Brig

Newcastle

Marston Moor

York   Hull

Irish Sea

North Sea

Naseby

Worcester

Edgehill

N

Oxford

Bristol   London

Dover

0	500	1000 Miles

0	800	1600 Kilometres

mons protested against James's foreign policy in these words:

> The Liberties, Franchises, Privileges and jurisdictions [freedom, rights and power] of Parliament are the ancient and undoubted birthright and inheritance of the subjects of England . . . the arduous and urgent affairs concerning the king, state and defence of the realm and of the Church of England, and the maintenance and making of laws, . . . are the proper subjects and matter of comment and debate in Parliament.

What James Thought of Parliament's Rights

Here is the House of Commons claiming the rights and powers which James said belonged to him alone. This was such a direct challenge to James's power that James tore the page containing them from the Journal of the House of Commons. So the stage was set for the great struggle between King and Parliament which was to remain for the rest of the seventeenth century. The great question was, should the King rule as well as reign by himself or only by the advice and consent of Parliament?

Charles I and Parliament

The quarrel between King and Parliament grew worse when Charles I came to the throne in 1625. Parliament would not grant him the money from taxes which he needed to govern the country. Parliament refused this money because it mistrusted Charles's religious policies and his claim to supreme power. Charles dismissed Parliament in 1629, as he had the right to do. He had made this clear to an earlier House of Commons:

> Parliaments are altogether in my power for the calling, sitting and dissolution [ending]. Therefore, as I find the fruits of them to be good or evil, they are to continue or not to be.

A Question of Money

How could these powers to call and dismiss Parliaments help Charles? Charles found that he could just raise enough money without Parliament to govern the country. But if an emergency arose and he needed extra money then he would have to call a Parliament to set new taxes. He tried to raise money by setting new taxes in his own right. One judge declared that no Act of Parliament could:

> . . . bind the King not to command his subjects, their persons and goods . . . and money too.

John Hampden, an English country gentleman, fought a lawsuit against the Crown's raising of taxes without Parliament's consent. He lost—not surprisingly for Charles appointed the judges and could dismiss them whenever he wanted. It looked like the end of English liberties though more people grew reluctant to pay the taxes that the King levied on his own account.

Archbishop Laud and the Puritans

Tension between Charles and the Puritans grew through the actions of Archbishop Laud, Charles's chief religious advisor. Charles was deeply religious and devoted to the Church of England. He supported Laud's efforts to reduce the influence of the Puritans. Laud persecuted the Puritans who hated him, a hatred which soon spread to include Charles. The years between 1629 and 1640 when Charles ruled without Parliament were called the 'Eleven Years' Tyranny' by the Puritans. Meanwhile in Scotland, apparently so peaceful, tiny clouds appeared which eventually grew into a storm.

Charles and the Scottish Kirk

Charles wanted to help the Scottish Kirk, in his view, by bringing it nearer to the Church of England in its services. He genuinely wanted to see more money going into the Kirk. He used his power of Revocation to recall into his hands all the land that had been taken by non-churchmen since 1540, before the Reformation. Since most of this land had been seized by the nobility and lairds, Charles angered this powerful group of people. They allied themselves with the Presbyterians who were suspicious of Charles's attempts to make the Kirk more Anglican. An alliance was formed which James VI would have been clever enough to prevent. In the end Charles was unable to buy up the lands he had recalled and so he gained nothing, but had lost the loyalty of the Scottish nobility. As a shrewd commentator, Sir James Balfour later wrote:

> [The Revocation] . . . was in effecte the ground-stone of all the mischiefe that followed after, both to this Kinges gouernment and family; and

The high &
mighty Monarch.
CHARLES by y.e grace
of GOD king of Great
Brittaine France &
Ireland Defendor of
the Fayth. etc.

EDYNBURGH

Co: v. Dalen sculp:

Charles I outside Edinburgh

whoeuer were the contriuers of it, deserue ther posterity [descendants] to be reputted [cursed] by thir three kingdomes, infamous and accursed for euer . . . [it led] to the alienatione [separation] of the subjects hartes from ther prince, and layed opin a way to rebellion. . .

We can see that Sir James was a Royalist but even he must have seen that Charles I was the main 'contriuer' of the whole sorry business.

Charles and Edinburgh

Charles visited his Scottish capital in 1633, a visit that cost Edinburgh £40 000 (Scots). Charles created a new Bishopric of Edinburgh and made St Giles the Bishop's Cathedral. The congregation of St Giles had to find a new kirk, and so the Tron Kirk was built at a cost of £14 000 (Scots) to a city that was already deeply in debt. This made Charles unpopular with the citizens of Edinburgh which was also a stronghold of Presbyterianism. His next action caused resentment and revolt.

The Prayer-Book Riot

You probably remember how James VI had cautiously refrained from imposing an Anglican-style Prayer Book on the Scottish Kirk. Charles I was either more sincere or more foolish than his father. Urged on by Archbishop Laud, he commanded the use of the Prayer Book in Scottish kirks. Charles never seemed to understand that the Scots felt as strongly about their Kirk as he did about the Anglican Church. The Scots were ordered to:

> . . . Conform themselves to the said public form of worship [the Prayer Book], which is the only form which we (having taken the counsel of our clergy) think fit to be used in God's public worship in this our kingdom.

This was a direct royal command and people noticed that Charles had not consulted the General Assembly of the Kirk nor the Scottish Estates.

The Covenanters

The Scots were convinced that their Kirk was in danger and that Charles would use armed force against whoever resisted or disobeyed his wishes. In February 1638 a National Covenant was drawn up. It was a truly 'national' statement. Thousands of Scots from nobleman to peasant signed the Covenant by which they swore:

> That we shall defend the same [religion] . . . and to the uttermost of power that God hath put in our hands, all the days of our life: and in like manner with the same heart, we declare before God and Men, That we have no intention nor desire to attempt anything that may turn to the dishonour of God, or to the diminution [lessening] of the Kingis greatness and authority . . .

It soon became clear that the 'Covenanters' would not just be satisfied with getting rid of the Prayer

The riot in St Giles. People brought their own stools to the service

Archibald Johnston of Warriston

Book but also wanted to get rid of the bishops as well. Archibald Johnston of Warriston was one of the drafters of the National Convenant and he wrote in his Journal on 4 May 1638:

> The Lord has led us hitherto by the hand fra step to step; and, at every step we wad haive stoodin at, made our adversaries to refuise and forced us to goe up a neu step of reformation ... not to settle til we speake plaine treuth according to the will of God, that is the utter overthrou and ruyne of Episcopacie [Bishops], that great grandmother of all our corruptions, innovations, usurpations, diseases and troubles.

Strong and determined language indeed!

Blue Bonnets over the Border

The Covenanters realised that words would soon give way to swords once the King could raise an army. So while Charles played for time the Covenanters raised an army from all over the Lowlands for, as the Covenanter Alexander Henderson said:

> Except we stand fast to our liberty we can look for nothing but miserable and perpetual slavery.

Henderson's words were to be heard more and more in the future. Volunteers for the Covenanting army came in quickly and the army was strengthened by the return of Scottish officers who had served under Gustavus Adolphus, the King of Sweden, in the Thirty Years War that was raging in Europe.

Covenanting Demands

The Covenanters did not wait for Charles but marched over the Border and captured Newcastle. There they waited and threatened to cut off London's coal supplies until Charles met their demands. The Scots wanted their religion guaranteed and for Charles to meet all the expenses which had been accrued for the upkeep of the Scottish army. Charles was faced by a huge bill and was determined to crush the Scots. To do these things he required money and this could only come from one place—Parliament.

Charles Summons Parliament

In November Charles summoned the 'Long' Parliament, so called because it lasted such a long time. This Parliament was determined to cut the King's power and 'purify' the Church of England. It realised that as long as a Scottish army remained in England Charles could not dismiss it. The result was a bitter struggle between King and Parliament. A revolt in Ireland needed an army to put it down but the great question of who was to lead it came up. Charles demanded the command as his but Parliament feared that this army might be turned against it. Charles tried to arrest five leaders who opposed him in the Commons and when this failed he set up his headquarters in Oxford. The Civil War had begun.

The Civil War

Charles led his armies towards London, the centre of Parliamentary opposition. The Royalists and Parliamentarians fought their first battle at Edgehill in November 1642. Though Charles won, the London militiamen still stood between him and London. Both sides sought allies—and the Covenanters had a fine army. Parliament agreed to the Scot's demands. It paid them for the Scottish army and by the Solemn League and Covenant of 1643 said it would:

> ... endeavour to bring the Churches of God in the three Kingdoms [Scotland, England and Ireland] to the nearest conjunction and uniformity [as close as possible] in Religion ... [and] form of Church-government...

You can see that the Covenanters wanted Parliament to force Presbyterianism on the English.

Charles II having his nose held to the grindstone.
He was forced to become a Covenanter to gain the
support of the Scots

The Covenanters Help to Defeat Charles

The Covenanters' army was soon in action alongside
Parliament's troops which included Oliver Cromwell's 'Ironsides'. Together they defeated the King's
armies at Marston Moor and Naseby. Charles surrendered to the Scots but they handed him over to
Parliament—like Judases for money said the Royalists. Charles was put on trial for treason and declared
guilty by a Parliamentary Court. He was executed on
a cold January afternoon in 1649. Philip Henry an
Oxford student watched the execution:

> I stood among the crowd in the street before
> Whitehall gate where the scaffold was erected
> and saw what was done, but was not so near as
> to hear anything. The blow I saw given, and can
> truly say with a sad heart, at the instant whereof,
> I remember well, there was such a groan by the
> thousands then present as I never heard before
> and desire I may never hear again.

Shortly afterwards the monarchy and the House
of Lords as well as the bishops were abolished—
England was now a Republican Commonwealth.
James VI's prophecy at Hampton Court had come
true.

Charles II, the Covenanting King

The Covenanters were angry because the English Parliament had not carried out the terms of the Solemn
League and Covenant. Charles I's son declared himself a Covenanter and was declared King Charles II
by the Scots who now tried to impose their new King
and religion on the English. Their attempts proved
futile for they were severely defeated by Cromwell at
the battle of Dunbar on 3 September 1650 and at
Worcester exactly a year later. Charles II narrowly
escaped capture and fled to the Continent.

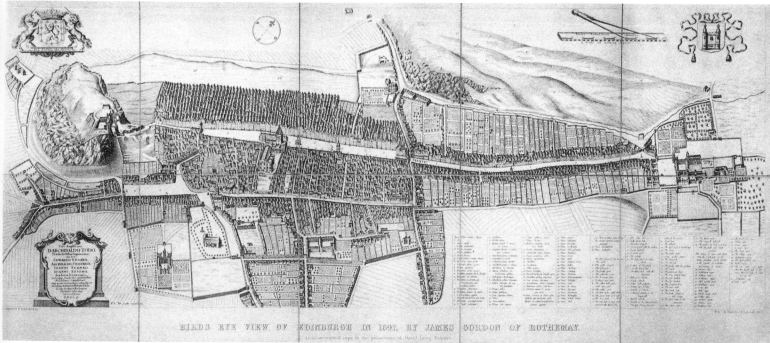

BIRDS EYE VIEW OF EDINBURGH IN 1647, BY JAMES GORDON OF ROTHEMAY.

The layout of Edinburgh in the mid-seventeenth century

The execution of Charles I

A cannon cast
in 1642

A United Commonwealth

Scotland became part of the Commonwealth and for the first time Scotland and England were really united when Scottish M.P.s met with their English counterparts in London. The Scots did not like the Commonwealth's rule though they had to admit it was fair if strict. For once peace reigned on both sides of the Highland line. As one man said:

> A man may ride all over Scotland with a switch [riding-stick] in his hand and £100 in his pocket, which he could not have done these five hundred years.

The King is Restored

Cromwell died in 1658 on the anniversary of his victories at Dunbar and Worcester. Two years of confusion followed until Charles II was restored. A 'Cavalier' or Royalist Parliament was elected which tried to put things back to what they were before the Long Parliament. In Scotland the power of the nobility was restored as was the Committee of the Articles. The King once more reigned supreme backed by a nobility who had not enjoyed their alliance with the Covenanters and their dangerous ideas of the equality of all

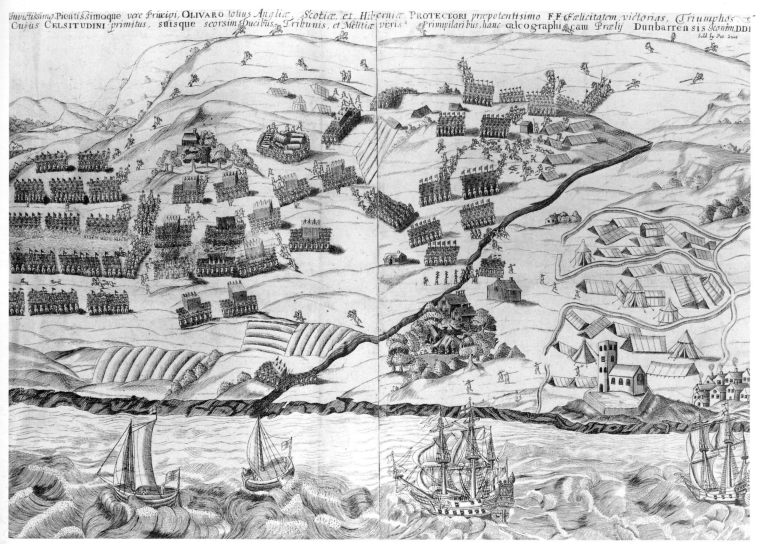

The Battle of Dunbar, September 3rd 1650

Charles II being crowned at Scone

men before God. Bishops were also brought back but they were to keep out of politics and rule as mildly as they had done in James VI's time. The use of the Prayer Book was left to the choice of each congregation. About 270 Covenanting ministers who did not agree with the restoration of bishops were evicted from the churches.

The Killing Times

These Covenanting ministers then began to hold 'conventicles', open-air meetings of which the Government strongly disapproved. Acts were passed against the conventicles and Government troops under General Tam Dalyell and Graham of Claverhouse hunted down the Covenanters. In 1678 the Government hit upon the idea of using Highlanders against the Covenanters and this made matters worse. The Covenanters fought back and though they had some successes they were defeated at the battles of Rullion

Green and Bothwell Brig. This period of transportation, persecution and execution of many Covenanters has been given the name 'The Killing Times'.

The Covenanters were called rebels by the Government, but no Covenanter could have accepted the terms of the Act of Supremacy of 1669 that:

> ... his Majestie, with advice and consent of his Estates of Parliament, doth heirby enact, assert and declare, that his Majestie hath the Supream Authority and Supremacie over all persons and in all causes ecclesiastical [religious] within this kingdom...

A New Catholic King

Charles II had once said that his brother James who was his heir would not reign for three years. Like most of the Stuarts James was brave but, unlike his

A conventicle

brother Charles, James was very sincere in his beliefs and rather stupid. When he was still Duke of York James became a Roman Catholic but was too honest to hide his religion in a violently anti-Catholic England. For his own safety James was sent by Charles to Scotland where he was well-liked as a person though the Scots were suspicious of his religion.

James Makes a Promise

When he became King in 1685 James II told his royal Council in England:

> I shall endeavour to preserve this government both in church and state as it is by law established. I know the principles of the Church of England are for monarchy and the members of it have shown themselves good and loyal subjects; therefore I shall always take care to defend and support it. I know too that the laws of England are sufficient to make the king as great a monarch as I wish; and as I shall never depart from the rights and prerogatives [privileges] of the crown, so shall I never invade any man's property.

These promises helped to quieten the fears of many people who did not see how it was possible for a Catholic King to defend the rights of the Protestant Church of England.

The Laws Against Catholics

James naturally wanted to help his fellow-Catholics by getting rid of all the laws which had been passed against them. Although most of the M.P.s were Royalists they were also devoted to the Church of England and did not want to repeal any laws against Catholics, Quakers and Presbyterians who were not members of the Church of England. Even the bishops in the House of Lords would find it difficult to remain loyal to James II if he tried to do away with the laws protecting the rights of the Anglican Church.

A Matter of the Royal Prerogative

Realising that Parliament would not repeal the laws against the Catholics James decided to do away with them himself by using his own prerogative or power as King. He passed an Act of Indulgence despite the promise he had made to his Council. In Scotland the Indulgence went like this:

> [We] ... do hereby give and grant by our royal toleration to the several professors [followers] of the Christian religion afternamed ... the moderate [non-Covenanting] Presbyterians ... in like manner do we tolerate Quakers ... [We] do

James II and VII when he was Duke of York

> therefore ... suspend, stop and disable all laws or acts of Parliament, customs or constitutions made or executed against any of our Roman Catholic subjects in any time past...

If the King can pass or do away with the laws without the consent of Parliament what need is there of a Parliament? Once more the old question arose; who is supreme, King or Parliament?

A Question of Toleration

Nowadays, we believe that everyone has the right to worship in his or her own way. In 1688, however, very few people believed in religious toleration. Most Scots and English thought that James's Indulgence was the first step to restoring the Pope's authority.

But there was something else that worried many people. James had passed a law:

> ... by our sovereign authority [over and above all other], prerogative royal and absolute power, which all our subjects are to obey without reserve [question].

It seemed as though James was putting the King's power beyond the reach of Parliament or people.

Bishops on Trial

James then ordered his Indulgence to be read from all church pulpits which was the best way of spreading public notices at that time. Seven Bishops of the Church of England refused to command their parsons to do this. James was very angry and put them on trial for treason. (He probably only wanted to make an example of them and intended setting them free by royal pardon if they had been found guilty.) Though many people were alarmed by his actions it is doubtful if they would have risen against James for they looked to the future. James was fifty-five, an old man for that time. His second wife, Mary of Modena, had had four children all of whom had died in infancy. People thought that James would be succeeded by his elder daughter, Mary, a devout Anglican who was married to the Protestant William of Orange the ruler of the Netherlands. Thus everyone thought that James's efforts to restore Catholicism would die with him.

A Prince is Born

But history is full of surprises. Mary of Modena gave birth to a healthy baby boy in June 1688. Some were so disappointed that they said another infant had been smuggled into the palace in a warming pan. There was great alarm when people realised that the infant Prince James would be reared as a Catholic and would continue his father's pro-Catholic policies into the future. In the midst of all this excitement the Seven Bishops were found not guilty and were released amidst widespread demonstrations of joy. On that same evening some of the most important men in England wrote to William of Orange pledging their support if he would invade England and remove James from power.

An Invasion is Launched

William's invasion fleet set sail and when he landed in England he received so much support that James fled to the protection of Louis XIV of France. People called this the 'Glorious Revolution' because it had saved the Church of England and the rule of Parliament. What made it more glorious was that no one had been killed.

The Revolution in Scotland

In Scotland a 'Convention' Estates met, called this because it had not been called by the King. By the Claim of Right in April 1689 the Convention declared bluntly that James VII was unfit to rule:

> Therefore the Estates of the Kingdom of Scotland, Find and Declare that King James the Seventh being a professed Papist, did assume the royal power, and acted as King, without ever taking the oath required by law, and hath by the advice of evil and wicked counsellours, invaded [overthrown] the fundamental constitution of the Kingdom, and altered it from a legal limited monarchy to an arbitrary despotick Power [dictatorship], and hath exercised the same, to the subversion [undermining] of the Protestant religions, and the violation of the laws and liberties of the Kingdom ... whereby he has forefaulted [forefeited] the right to the Crown ... and the Throne is become vacant.

As you can see the Claim of Right is a list of crimes which the Convention thought James had committed. It went on to declare:

> That the giving of gifts or grants, for raising of money without the consent of Parliament, or Convention of Estates is contrary to law.

By the Claim the office of bishop was also abolished and shortly afterwards the Presbyterian Kirk became the established or official Kirk of Scotland. This means that an Anglican king becomes a Presbyterian one as soon as he crosses the Border from England into Scotland!

The vacant throne was then offered to William and Mary who agreed to the Claim of Right.

The Committee of the Articles

Shortly afterwards Articles of Grievances were drawn up in Scotland. The first article stated:

> The Estates of the Kingdome of Scotland doe represent [maintain] that the committee of parliament called the Articles is a great grievance to the nation, and that there ought to be no committees of Parliament but such as are freely chosen by the estates...

The Estates Gain Independence

The abolition of the Committee of the Articles freed the Scottish Estates from the King's rule. For the first time in its history the Scottish Estates were independent. England and Scotland had now the same monarchs but they were two separate countries each with its own Parliament intensely jealous and proud of its hard-won independence.

Something To Remember

Most of this chapter is about *power* and who was going to wield that power. At the beginning of the seventeenth century most people in England and Scotland agreed that it was the King's duty to rule as well as reign. In England the King was also the Head of the Church, and in Scotland James VI had extended his control over the Kirk's affairs by the end of his reign. The English Parliament also recognised the King's right to rule but only if he did not try to do away with the laws which only Parliament could pass. This was the real cause of the quarrel between King and Parliament because the King said that if a law interfered with the wise ruling of the country then he had the right to ignore it.

In Scotland matters came to a head when Charles I tried to make the Kirk use a Prayer Book which the Scots thought was a threat to their way of worship. The Scottish Covenanters joined forces with those who supported the rights of the English Parliament. Charles I was defeated and executed and a republic replaced the monarchy. Eleven years later the monarchy was restored with great rejoicing because most people were tired of a military dictatorship.

When James II and VII used royal power to give freedom of worship to his fellow-Catholics, many feared that this would lead to the restoration of Roman Catholicism. Many others feared that here was the King trying to overrule Parliament. These two fears caused the Revolution of 1688. Both the Scottish and English Parliaments put forward claims to pass laws without royal interference and to prevent the King from changing laws passed by Parliament. By accepting these claims Mary and William agreed that future monarchs must rule according to Parliamentary laws.

Something to Think About

The quarrel between King and Parliament in Britain during the seventeenth century was important to the future of all mankind. It decided the vital question of who is to rule. Was it was to be a king, a dictator or a parliament, congress or an assembly which is chosen by the people to represent them? The victory of Parliament meant that in the future what Abraham Lincoln called, 'the rule of the people, by the people, for the people' would be a part of history. This kind of government which we call 'democracy' was not to come about straightaway in Britain and the rest of the world—it still does not exist in many parts of the world. However, by making sure that British monarchs would now have to rule according to the laws of Parliament it started the world on the road to democracy.

The Covenanters showed that the Scottish people were determined to defend their way of worshipping —even if it meant rebelling against royal power. At a time when royal power was increasing all over Europe this was an outstanding example of a people refusing to worship the way its ruler wanted it to do. However, it must be noticed that the Covenanters were not eager to give other people the right to worship in their own way. The Covenanters would have said that because the Presbyterian form of religion was the best, then people should not be allowed to choose the second-best. In this way they resemble many modern political parties. You will probably have your own ideas about these arguments.

Massacre at Glencoe

A Highland Raid

One of the supporters of James II and VII was John Graham Viscount Dundee—nicknamed 'Bonnie Dundee'. Dundee gathered a Highland army and defeated a Convention army at Killiecrankie in July 1689. In his moment of victory Dundee was killed. The Covenanters who hated him said that Dundee had been shot by a silver bullet which was the only way to kill someone who was in league with the Devil.

After the death of Bonnie Dundee his Highland supporters began to return to their homes. On their way back the MacDonalds of Glencoe and their kinsmen of Keppoch followed the ancient and honourable custom of raiding the lands of their enemies. They plundered Glenorchy the home of John Campbell, first Earl of Breadalbane, because he had stayed at home instead of coming 'out' for King James. This was not the first time the men of Glencoe had raided Campbell territory but the great raid of 1689 was the worst of them all.

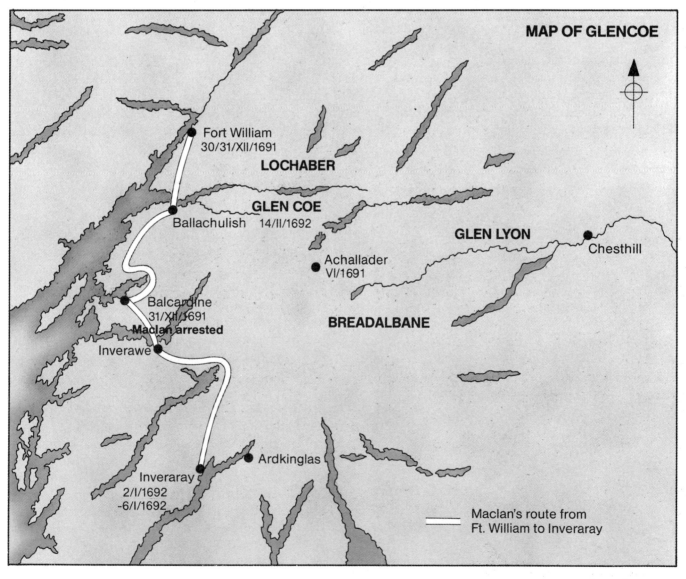

MAP OF GLENCOE

Fort William
30/31/XII/1691

LOCHABER

GLEN COE
Ballachulish   14/II/1692

GLEN LYON

Chesthill

Achallader
VI/1691

Balcardine
31/XII/1691
Maclan arrested

BREADALBANE

Inverawe

Ardkinglas

Inveraray
2/I/1692
-6/I/1692

—— Maclan's route from
Ft. William to Inveraray

The Campbell who suffered most was Robert Campbell of Glenlyon. He was already so deeply in debt through drinking and gambling that this house at Chesthill had been put in his wife's name to stop him from selling it. In one afternoon what little property he had left was lifted by the MacDonalds; his few sheep, cattle, goats and his splendid brown stallion worth £200 Scots. His home was plundered and even the kitchen utensils carried off to Glencoe. Glenlyon was forced to borrow money and become a soldier at the age of sixty. Through his family connections with the Earl of Argyll, the chief of Clan Campbell, he was made a captain in the newly formed Earl of Argyll's Regiment.

Glenlyon's Revenge

At five o'clock on Saturday 13 February 1692, Glenlyon gave orders to his men to kill as many Mac-Donalds of Glencoe as they could. For twelve days Glenlyon and his men had been the guests of the MacDonalds but when the killing was finished that day MacIan of Glencoe and thirty-seven of his clan lay dead.

Robert Campbell of Glenlyon

Who was Responsible?

When it is written like that it looks as though Glenlyon and his men were totally responsible for the massacre of the MacDonalds of Glencoe. However, when we act like historians and examine the evidence of the events which led up to the Massacre we discover that many other men were equally responsible. We will follow a trail of guilt that leads us right back to King William III himself. The first step will be to find out who gave Glenlyon his orders and who it was that sent him to Glencoe.

Troublesome Highlanders

We can begin our investigations in the year 1681. In that year James Duke of York, Charles II's brother, issued a Proclamation to check the lawlessness of the Highlanders. The Proclamation ordered all the Highland chiefs to come to Edinburgh and swear an oath that they and their clansmen would keep the peace. To give force to the Proclamation, the Government sent soldiers into the Highlands to punish anyone who did not swear the oath. You can see that the Stuart Kings had no more liking for the wild Highlanders than the Lowlanders had. The Stuart rulers used to deal brutally with the Highlanders, except when the clansmen could be useful to them. As for the Highlanders, they felt no more loyalty to the Stuarts than they would have had for any king in Edinburgh or London. In 1681 one of the chiefs who swore loyalty was MacIan of Glencoe, aged nearly sixty, a giant of a man, 6'7" tall with great white mustachios swept back behind his ears. MacIan charmed all he met with his hospitality and his fine Highland courtesy.

James Uses the Highlanders
The Duke of York eventually became King James II and VII and in 1685 he called out the clans to put down the rebellious Campbell Earl of Argyll. Argyll was defeated and lost his head on the Maiden, the Scottish guillotine. A Highland host was let loose to plunder and rape its way through Campbell territory. The Campbells were hated and feared for the way they had taken other clans' lands and so many old scores were paid off.

William Replaces James

When James fled the country in 1688 his daughter Mary and son-in-law, William III took the throne. Most of the Highland chiefs supported James, perhaps because he was too far away in France to interfere with them. William III cared little for England and even less for Scotland. He wanted to use the wealth of these countries and their manpower for the defence of his beloved Holland against the might of Louis XIV of France. He could not do this if some troublesome Highland chiefs still remained loyal to James, Louis's ally. As far as William was concerned the Highlanders would have to remain peaceful—and loyal.

John Dalrymple, Master and later Earl of Stair

The Master of Stair

William had the man to ensure this. John Dalrymple, Master of Stair, was one of William's Secretaries for Scotland. Stair was hard-working, clever and ambitious. He knew if he could achieve a lasting peace in the Highlands he would keep William's favour. Like most Lowlanders of this time he regarded the majority of Highlanders as nothing more than treacherous, troublesome, barbarous cattle-thieves and robbers. To Stair there was a simple solution to the Highland problem: use force. Stair did not often lose his temper; when he did so it was usually because he thought the Highlanders were misbehaving. At these times Stair was dangerous, ruthless and deadly.

'As Cunning as a Fox . . .'

John Campbell, Earl of Breadalbane, suggested to Stair another way to deal with the Highlanders. It was a simple plan. As a Highland chief himself Campbell would meet the chiefs, persuade them to give up their loyalty to James and become William's men. To do this he would need money as well as words; Breadalbane thought £12 000 would be sufficient.

John Campbell, Earl of Breadalbane

His own ambition was simple and magnificent; to make himself Chief of Clan Campbell, above or at least equal to 'Mac Cailein Mor', Earl of Argyll. Charles II had once said;

> There was never trouble brewing in Scotland but that a Dalrymple or a Campbell was at the bottom of it.

Now here was a Campbell who had been called:

> Cunning as a fox, wise as a serpent, slippery as an eel. No government can trust him but where his private [own] interest is in view.

This Campbell was now working with a Dalrymple.

A Meeting and a Quarrel
Breadalbane invited many Highland chiefs to his castle at Achallader in June 1691. During a week of games and feasting he took aside the chiefs one by one and, by a mixture of flattery, promises and threats, got most of them to swear loyalty to William. However, these proud men would only agree to this if James VII released them from their oath of loyalty to him; it was a matter of honour. MacIan of Glencoe refused to promise and quarrelled with Breadalbane. Perhaps it was MacIan's remark that he could not trust a man who was William's man in Edinburgh and James's in the Highlands that led to the quarrel. MacIan told his sons:

> There's bad blood between our family and his. I fear mischief from no man so much as the Earl of Breadalbane.

Stair Grows Impatient
Breadalbane was anxious to make his plan succeed and his anxiety must have grown when he received a letter from Stair:

> You will see that he [William III] has stopped all hostilities against the Highlanders till he may hear from you ... but if they will be mad, before Lammas [1 August], they will repent it, for the army will be allowed to go into the Highlands, which some so much thirst for ...

About this time Breadalbane also suggested that force might be used to back up bribery. This idea met with Stair's approval, though he was careful afterwards to say it had been Breadalbane's idea.

An Oath of Allegiance

In August 1691 Stair persuaded William to issue a Proclamation which stated that all those who had borne arms against William were to swear an oath of allegiance to him before the sheriff of the shire in which they lived. This had to be sworn by 1 January 1692:

> ... and such as shall continue obstinate and incorrigible [unwilling to mend their ways], after this Gracious offer of Mercy, shall be punished as Traytors and Rebels, and otherways to the utmost extremity of the Law. . . .

The Chiefs Delay
You can imagine Stair's anger when none of the chiefs came forward to swear the oath. Though many of them feared William's anger, they were still James's men until they were released from their oath. So their fate rested in the unsure hands of James, whose thoughts were more on the next world than this one. Always a ditherer, James's indecision was now to prove fatal for the MacDonalds. Time passed and still James came to no decision. Meanwhile, Stair sent Lieutenant-Colonel Hamilton to be Deputy-governor at Fort William knowing that Hamilton would carry out any order Stair gave him. Breadalbane was also growing impatient. He wrote to one of his stewards:

> ... and they [the chiefs] talk as if they were to give terms and not to receive them, but they will find that a great mistake in a few weeks ...

It is difficult to know whether Breadalbane knew what was going to happen, or if he was only guessing.

Stair Prepares
At the beginning of December there was still no word from James. Stair wrote to Hamilton; a strange letter in which he mixed flattery and threats:

> ... It may be that shortly we may have use of your garrison, for the winter time is the only season in which we are sure the Highlanders cannot escape us, nor carry their wives, bairns and cattle to the mountains.

It shows the lines along which Stair's thoughts were running. It also shows how ignorant he was of the hardiness of the Highlanders. Two days later he wrote to Hamilton again:

> . . . and since the Government cannot oblige them [the chiefs], it's obliged to receive some of them and to weaken and frighten the rest. The MacDonalds will fall into this net. That's the only popish clan in the kingdom, and it will be popular to take a severe course with them. Let me hear from you with the first [post?] whether you think this is the proper season to maul them in the long cold nights . . . and [you] must be ready by the first of January.

It is quite possible that Stair had the MacDonalds of Glengarry in mind rather than those at Glencoe. About this time Stair wrote to Breadalbane mentioning, '. . . your scheme for mauling them'.

Release from James's Allegiance

James finally signed the release on 12 December 1691. It took the messenger only nine days to go from Paris to Edinburgh. It was not until 28 December that the news reached the Highlands. The next day 400 men of Argyll's Regiment left for Fort William.

Trouble for MacIan of Glencoe

The pace of events now hots up. On 30 December, Colonel Hill, the commander of the garrison at Fort William was astonished and angry when MacIan appeared to take the oath. He explained that MacIan would have to swear the oath before Campbell of Ardkinglas, the Sheriff of Argyll. Hill knew MacIan had not made a mistake in appearing before him but that the thought of taking the oath before a Campbell at Inverary was more than MacIan's pride could swallow. Patiently, Hill said that Ardkinglas was a just and honest man and he gave MacIan a letter to the Sheriff asking him to receive MacIan like a lost sheep.

MacIan at Inverary

Struggling south to Inverary in bad weather, MacIan and his two servants were arrested by Captain Drummond who was leading an advance party of Argyll's Regiment. Drummond was a Lowlander, naturally suspicious of wandering Highland chiefs and he paid no attention to Colonel Hill's letter. MacIan was held prisoner for a day which was to prove fatal for him

and his clan. He reached Inverary on 2 January and heard the chilling news that Ardkinglas was away visiting his family at New Year. Ardkinglas returned on 5 January and at first refused to hear MacIan take the oath as the Proclamation had made 1 January the deadline. Ardkinglas relented when he saw tears running down MacIan's face and the chief took the oath the following day. Although he rebuked MacIan for being late, Ardkinglas sent Hill's letter along with his own recommendation for mercy to the King's Council in Edinburgh. When MacIan returned to Glencoe he told his clan that they were now under the safe protection of King William.

Stair Acts

At first Stair heard that MacIan had taken the oath, but as some others had not, he decided to make an example of them. He wrote to General Livingstone who commanded the Army in Scotland ordering him:

> . . . to act against those Highland rebels who have not taken the benefit of our indemnity [pardon], by fire and sword and all manner of hostility: to burn their houses, seize or destroy their goods or cattle, plenishings [furnishings] or clothes, and to cut off the men . . .

William made this a royal command by signing at the top and bottom of the page. Later that evening Stair received word that MacIan had not taken the oath on time and he added a conclusion to the letter:

> Just now my Lord Argyll tells me that Glencoe hath not taken the oaths, at which I rejoice. It's a great work of charity to be exact in rooting out the damnable sept [clan], the worst in all the Highlands.

Notice Stair's mention of Argyll.

On 16 January 1692 Stair wrote to Livingstone again, the last clause of his instructions stated quite clearly:

> If M'Kean [MacIan] of Glencoe, and that tribe, can be well separated from the rest, it will be a proper vindication [a just end] of the public justice to extirpate [to destroy totally] that sept of thieves.

Once more William III signed the page. Later, Stair wrote to Colonel Hill with instructions about how to

seal the entrances to Glencoe and cut off any escaping MacDonalds.

By 30 January Stair had learnt the truth, that Mac-Ian had signed the oath but six days late. That was enough for Stair's lawyer-mind for he wrote to Livingstone that day:

> I am glad that Glencoe did not come in within the time prescribed . . . I think to harry their cattle or burn their houses is but to render them desperate, lawless men, to rob their neighbours; but I believe you will be satisfied it were [would be] of great advantage to the nation that thieving tribe were rooted out and cut off. It must be quietly done, otherwise they will make shift for both men and cattle [both will escape].

'Do not Trouble the Government with Prisoners'

When Livingstone in Edinburgh received this letter, he wrote immediately to Hamilton at Fort William:

> So, Sir, here is a fair occasion for you to show that your garrison serves for some use . . . I desire you to begin with Glencoe, and spare nothing that belongs to him, but do not trouble the Government with prisoners.

That last sentence is very chilling.

Hamilton ordered two companies of Argyll's Regiment to march to Glencoe. They were under the command of Captain Robert Campbell of Glenlyon.

Arrival at Glencoe

The soldiers arrived at Glencoe on 1 February. Mac-Ian's son John was suspicious at first but Glenlyon quietened his fears by saying that the garrison at Fort William was overcrowded and asking for shelter for a few days for himself and his men. Glenlyon and his men were warmly welcomed to Glencoe. All enmity between Campbell and MacDonald was forgotten.

At Fort William, Hill was reluctant to sign the orders for which Hamilton impatiently waited. On 12 February, Hill received a final letter from Stair. Stair's instructions were short and to the point: 'Let it be secret and sudden.'

Hill ordered Hamilton to march to Glencoe with 400 men and 400 of Argyll's Regiment under the command of Major Duncanson. Hamilton wrote to Duncanson ordering him to be in position by 7am on Saturday 14 and to be sure:

> . . . that the old fox and none of his cubs get away. The orders are that none be spared, nor the government be troubled with prisoners.

'Fall upon the Rebells'

On receiving this message, Duncanson immediately sent orders to Glenlyon at Glencoe. His messenger was the same Captain Drummond who had earlier arrested MacIan. Glenlyon received these orders:

> *Sir,*
>   You are hereby ordered to fall upon the Rebells, the MacDonalds of Glencoe, and put all to the sword under seventy. You are to have speciall care that the old ffox and his sones doe upon no account escape your hands. You are to secure all the avenues [paths] that no man escape. This you are to putt in execution at fyve of the clock precisely; and by that time or verie shortly after it, Ile [I'll] strive to be att you with a stronger party: if I doe not come to you att fyve, you are not to tary [wait] for me, but to fall on . . . See that this be putt in execution without feud or favour, else you may expect to be dealt with as one not true to King or Government, nor a man fitt to cary Commissions in the Kings service. Expecting you will not faill in the fulfilling hereof, as you love yourself . . .

This extract contains many important points about the Massacre. Notice that Duncanson put forward the hour to begin the attack, from 7am to 5am. In fact Duncanson did arrive at 7am. It appears as if he was trying to make sure he could not be blamed for starting the slaughter. Duncanson also threatens Glenlyon if the orders are not carried out 'without feud or favour'. Glenlyon would lose his commission and his pay of 8/- (0.40p) a day, his total means of livelihood. One other important point to notice is that this was the first time Glenlyon knew why he had been sent to Glencoe.

Orders are Obeyed

Whether he was surprised or not by these orders, Glenlyon passed them on to his Lieutenant and sergeants. The private soldiers were not told until they were lined up before five the next morning. There are stories that some of the Campbell soldiers tried to warn the MacDonalds when they heard of the outrage to the Highland hospitality they had received. There was much movement, and whispered messages were drowned in the rising snowstorm. John MacDonald awakened and went to see Glenlyon who was up and armed. Glenlyon said that he had received orders to march to new quarters. MacDonald returned to his home unharmed—it was not yet five o'clock!

The Massacre

The action began promptly at five. A swirling blizzard muffled the sounds of shots and hid the fires of burning cottages. MacIan was awakened and thinking the soldiers were leaving his glen, he stumbled half-dressed to give them the parting drink of whisky. It was his last act of hospitality—he was shot at the side of his bed and his body dragged out into the snow. His wife was spared but the soldiers ripped off her rings with their teeth before casting her into the blizzard. MacIan and thirty-seven of his clan were killed that morning. John MacDonald and his brother Alisdair escaped in the blizzard which hid them and delayed Hamilton's men from blocking off the passes. The bare mountains and the harsh weather killed more of the youngest and oldest of the clan. Duncanson arrived later and was furious with Glenlyon for allowing MacIan's sons to escape.

The News Leaks Out

Several weeks passed before the Massacre became generally known. Stair's attitude is shown quite clearly in a letter he wrote to Hill:

> It's true that the affair of Glencoe was very ill-executed, but 'tis strange to me that means so much regret for such a sept of thieves.

A few days after the Massacre one of Breadalbane's servants tracked down the MacDonald brothers who were still in hiding. He proposed that if they would declare Breadalbane's innocence of the killings then he would try to obtain a pardon for them from William. Breadalbane, the fox, had smelled something nasty in the wind from Glencoe.

A Royal Commission Reports

In 1695 a Royal Commission was set up to investigate the Massacre. At that time the Scottish Estates were hostile to William III and his ministers. The Commission declared that William was innocent because he had had no knowledge of the plans for the Massacre! Many members of the Commission were enemies of Stair, so it is not surprising that he was found responsible along with others. The Estates were blunter when they declared that he was: 'the original cause of this unhappy business'.

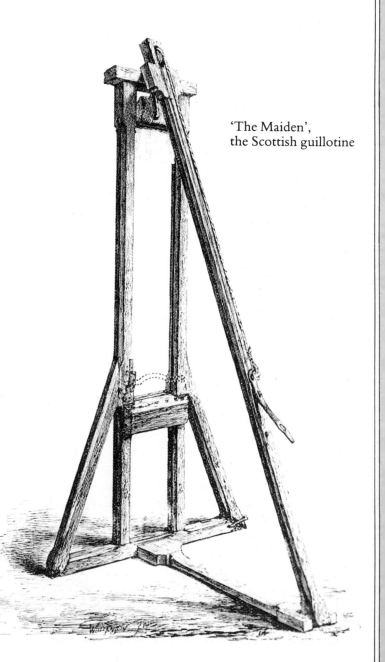

'The Maiden', the Scottish guillotine

Breadalbane, with no friends and many enemies, was imprisoned in Edinburgh Castle terrified by thoughts of being the Maiden's next victim. He was not imprisoned in connection with the Massacre but for having entered into treasonable talks with the chiefs at Achallader.

Colonel Hill was declared innocent; probably a true verdict. Livingstone was cleared with the help of his supporters although he had known about the plans in advance. Duncanson, Glenlyon, Drummond and several others were found guilty as being, '. . . actors in the slaughter of the Glencoe men under trust'. The Estates asked for them to be sent back from Flanders where they were serving in William's army. William did not do this, he had more use for Scottish soldiers than sending them home to stand trial. Hamilton refused to appear before the Commission and remained safely in Ireland. The MacDonalds asked for compensation for the goods and cattle looted at Glencoe. They got nothing.

Who Was To Blame?

If the soldiers who had carried out the Massacre had been put on trial they would have said they were only obeying orders. Hew Dalrymple, Stair's younger brother, said that Livingstone and all the soldiers who took part in the Massacre were to blame, because:

> Though the command of superior officers be very absolute [strong and complete], yet no commands against the laws of nature be binding: so that a soldier retaining his commission, ought to refuse to execute any barbarity, as if a soldier could be commanded to shoot a man passing by, inoffensively [harmlessly] upon the street, no such command would exempt him from punishment of murder.

In Our Own Century

Our own century shows that the excuse of obeying orders is not always regarded as an excuse for murder. Adolf Eichmann claimed that he had been obeying orders when he sent thousands of Jews to the gas-chambers of Nazi concentration camps. An Israeli court refused to accept Eichmann's plea and he was executed in 1962. Lieutenant William Calley was dismissed from the U.S. Army and imprisoned for murdering Vietnamese villagers whom he had sus-

William III

pected of sheltering enemy guerillas. The U.S. court refused to accept his plea that his conduct was normal practice in dealing with such suspects.

Perhaps Stair should not be held totally to blame. No one at the time believed that William III knew nothing of the plans. In any case, Stair would have never dared to send the instructions without William's permission. Perhaps James VII shares in the responsibility for his delay in releasing the chiefs from their loyalty to him in time. Perhaps even the MacDonalds were responsible. They had made too many enemies in the past by their raids and MacIan had had over three months to swear the oath.

Perhaps you would like to consider who was most guilty.

John Graham of Claverhouse, 'Bonnie Dundee'

Problems for the Estates

After the Revolution of 1689 the new, independent Scottish Estates or parliament faced a number of serious problems. The first was how to deal with the 'Jacobites' as the supporters of James VII were now called. The Jacobites were determined to replace the 'Parliamentary' rulers, William and Mary, and restore 'the King over the water' to the throne which they thought was rightfully his. As you have seen, a civil war broke out and the Jacobites under 'Bonnie Dundee' won a victory at Killiecrankie which was to bring him glory and death. With his death the heart went out of the Highlanders whom he had led to victory. The Estates and King William's government were able to breathe easily again.

Highland Massacres

The rule of the Government at Edinburgh was always weak in the west and north of the Highlands and the Massacre of Glencoe (you read about it in *Case History 3*) shows how much the Estates' laws were obeyed in the Highlands. The fact that the Massacre had been planned and ordered in London made members of the Estates fear that the bad old days of

TIME-LINE 1688-1707

1688 — James VII & II flees to France. Convention Estates in Scotland. Revolution Settlements in Scotland and England.

1689 — Battle of Killiecrankie. Death of Dundee. Battle of Dunkeld.

1692 — Massacre of Glencoe.

1695 — Darien Company Founded.

} The 'Ill Years'.

1700 — English Parliament passes Act of Succession. Electors of Hanover named as future rulers of England.

1701 — James VII & II dies. Louis XIV recognises James Edward Stuart as King of Britain.

1702 — William III dies. Anne queen. War breaks out with France.

1703 — Scottish Estates pass Act Anent Peace & War.

1704 — Estates pass Act of Security.

1705 — *Worcester* Incident. English Parliament passes Alien's Act.

1706 — Delegates from Scotland & England meet to discuss Union.

1707 — Treaty of Union signed.

the Committee of the Articles had returned and that Scotland was once more ruled by the King's Court in London. This was one of the reasons why many Lowland Scots were aroused by the Massacre as their normal feelings towards the Highlanders were a mixture of fear, contempt and hostility.

Scotland's Greatest Problem

The greatest problem of all facing the Scots was the poorness of their country. What made it worse was that while Scotland appeared to become poorer and poorer, England seemed to grow richer. By the end of the seventeenth century the Scottish pound was only worth one-twelfth of the English pound sterling. To add to this there were crop failures for several years in succession. Many said that the failure of the harvests was God's punishment on a sinful people. This was written by a minister, Patrick Walker:

> These unheard-of manifold Judgments continued seven Years, not always alike, but the Seasons, Summer and Winter, so cold and barren ... Meal became so scarce, that ... many could not get it. It was not then with many, 'Where will we get Silver?' but 'Where shall we get Meal for Silver?' I have seen, when all the meal was sold in the markets, Women clapping their Hands, and tearing the clothes off their Heads crying, 'How shall we go home and see our Children die in hunger? They have got no Meal these two days, and we have nothing to give them.'
> Through the long Continuance of these manifold Judgments, Deaths and Burials were so many and so common, that the living were weary of Burying of the Dead.

Notice that Patrick Walker's language is very like that of the Old Testament, even unto the seven years of famine. Notice also how customs change for in those days people expressed their grief by 'clapping their Hands'.

Why Were the Scots So Poor?
Even the most devout Scots must have wondered at God's mysterious ways when He made the godly Scots poor and the not-so-godly English rich. Many Scots thought that there were other reasons, not divine, why there were such differences in wealth between the two countries. They said that England possessed overseas colonies and that trade with these colonies was the main reason for England's wealth.

Scotland had no colonies. Besides, when the Commonwealth had ended in 1660 the English refused to allow the Scots to trade with the English colonies and treated the Scots like any other foreigners, even though they had the same monarchs.

A Scheme to Make Scotland Rich

One way to make Scotland richer was for the Estates to set up 'The Company of Scotland Trading to Africa and the Indies'. This was done in 1695 and things went well at first for even English merchants subscribed money for the Company. But the rich and powerful English East India Company complained to William III that the Company of Scotland would ruin their trade. At the same time the English Government ordered its colonies to stop giving help to the Scots. It looked as though the new Company was doomed.

Scottish Anger
The Scots were furious and decided to raise the money by themselves. Altogether the sum of £400 000 sterling was raised—a vast sum for such a poor country. The capital came from all kinds of people—small dealers in Edinburgh, the skippers of ships from Glasgow, from burgh councils. It was noticed that few Highland chiefs bought shares in the Company and very few of the 'great men' of Scotland appeared on the list of subscribers.

The Dream of William Paterson
One of the Directors of the Company was William Paterson, a man of great vision. Like some other Scots, Paterson had made his fortune in London as a merchant. In 1692 he had helped to form the Bank of England. Paterson wanted to use the Company to make Scotland one of the great trading nations of the world, like the English and Dutch. His scheme was to set up Scottish colonies on either side of the narrow neck of land in Central America near Panama which he called Darien. Goods would be transported across this isthmus between the towns of New Edinburgh and New St Andrews.

Darien
If you look at the map of Darien on page 81 you will see that this was a good spot for trading between the Atlantic and Pacific Oceans. In this way Paterson was two hundred years ahead of his time for that is

when the Panama Canal was built. The Scots were not going to build a canal but intended using pack-animals to transport goods. In another way Paterson was ahead of his time for he wanted all nations to trade freely with the Scottish colony and did not exclude foreign merchants as other European countries did.

Failure and English Opinion

In *Case History 4* you will see the reasons why the Darien Scheme failed. The Scots blamed English opposition for the failure of the Company and anti-English feeling grew even stronger. If the English thought of the Scots at all it was probably with contempt for a poor, half-savage people obsessed with religion. The few Scots that the English saw were sometimes the worst kind—courtiers on the make and traders trying to get rich quickly.

A Royal Succession

In 1702 William III died and was succeeded by Anne, the younger daughter of James II and VII by his first wife. Though Anne had had many children none had survived childhood. The great question was, who was going to succeed Anne? Her half-brother, James Edward the son of James II and VII, was a Catholic and the Revolution Settlement had laid down that no Catholic could succeed to the throne. In 1700 the English Parliament passed the Act of Settlement naming Sophia, the Protestant Electress of Hanover in Germany, and her descendants as heirs to the English Crown when Anne died.

War Breaks Out

In September 1701 when James II and VII died, Louis XIV of France recognised his son Prince James Edward Stuart as the King of Scotland and England. The English Parliament was so angry at Louis's interference that war broke out between the two countries in 1702. Both Scots and English did not trust Louis XIV because in 1685 he had taken away the right for French Protestants, or 'Huguenots' as they were called, to worship in their own way. Many Huguenots had escaped to Britain and brought with them a hatred of the French King.

Queen Anne can be seen at the centre of this painted ceiling at Hampton Court Palace

Scottish Opinion

But the Scots felt rather differently about all this. They reluctantly went to war with France because Queen Anne was their ruler. But the Scottish Estates were determined that in future no English Parliament was going to declare war for them. The Act Anent Peace and War of 1703 put it this way:

> That after Her Majesty's [Anne's] decease, and failyeing heirs of her body, no person being King or Queen of Scotland and England, shall have the sole power of making war with any Prince, Potentate [ruler] or State whatsomever without consent of Parliament [the Estates]; and that no Declaration of War without consent foresaid, shall be binding on the Subjects of this Kingdom [Scotland] . . .

Later in the same year the Estates followed this up with an Act allowing the import of foreign wine. No 'English' war was going to stop the Scots drinking the good red wine of France!

KINGS & QUEENS OF BRITAIN 1603-1760

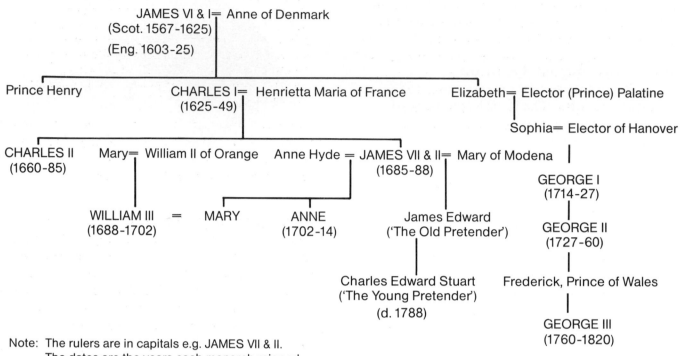

Note: The rulers are in capitals e.g. JAMES VII & II.
The dates are the years each monarch reigned.

An Act of Security

If these two acts annoyed the English government then much worse was to come with the Act of Security in 1704. This Act only received Anne's consent when the Estates refused to grant any money for the war until she agreed to it. The most important part of the Act stated that the Scottish Estates would choose the heir to the Scottish throne on Anne's death:

> Provided always, That the same be *not* Successor to the Crown of England [unless the] freedom, Frequency and Power of the Scottish Parliaments, the Religion, Liberty and Trade of the Nation from English or any Foreign Influence [was guaranteed].

Two Countries: Two Kings

Prince James Edward Stuart, the 'Old Pretender' was the one person who was free of any English 'Influence'. He had been banned from the English throne and was supported by Louis XIV, the enemy of the English. 'James VIII' had many Jacobite supporters in Scotland. Suddenly, the old fears of the English that the Scots would provide a convenient 'back-door' for a French invasion of England were revived. During the long and heated debates in the Scottish Estates when the Scottish supporters of Queen Anne's government were trying to destroy the Act of Security there was no doubt about the feelings of the Scottish people in general:

> ... there was nothing to be seen or heard ... but Jollity, Mirth, and a universal Satisfaction and Approbation [Approval] of what was done, and that by People of all Ranks and Degrees.

It looked as though the Scots were determined to gain revenge on the English for the failure of the Darien Scheme.

Hatred Boils Over

Then an incident occurred which brought Anglo-Scottish relations to an all-time low. The English ship *Worcester* sailed into the Forth for water and supplies. The Scots thought, wrongly as it happened, that the ship belonged to the hated East India Company which had done so much to destroy the Company of Scotland. An ugly rumour began to spread that Captain Green and the crew of the *Worcester* had pirated a Scottish ship, the *Speedy Return*, which was long overdue. Green and fourteen of his crew were put on trial, found guilty and sentenced to death by Scottish judges threatened by the Edinburgh mob. Queen Anne sent a pardon, saying that there was no real evidence to convict Green and his men. This was ignored and Green and two crew members were hanged on Leith sands. Some time later the rest of the *Worcester's* crew were released which looks as though the Scots felt guilty at the punishment of innocent men. If the crew was innocent, then so were the hanged men. It showed how easily the Scots could be led into murderous actions by their hatred of all things English.

The English Parliament Cracks a Whip

The English Parliament reacted swiftly. English public opinion was disgusted by the '*Worcester* Incident' and the Act of Security was seen as a direct threat to England in the middle of a war. To the English the Scots seemed ready to stab them in the back. Frightened and furious, the English Parliament struck back with the 'Aliens Act':

> An Act for the effectual securing of the kingdom of England from the apparent dangers that may arise from several acts lately passed by the parliament of Scotland.
>
> For preventing the many inconveniences which may speedily happen to the two Kingdoms of England and Scotland, *if a nearer and more compleat union be not made between the said Kingdoms* . . . that from and after the five and twentieth day of December [1705] no person or persons being a native or natives of the Kingdom of Scotland . . . shall enjoy any benefit or advantage of a natural born subject of England but every such person shall be from henceforth adjudged and taken as an alien . . . until such time as the succession to the Crown of Scotland be declared and settled by an Act of Parliament in Scotland in the same manner [as] the succession to the Crown of England is now settled . . .

The Act then went on to say that after 25 December no Scottish cattle, sheep, coal or linen would be allowed into England.

The Aliens Act was a warning and a threat to the Scots. They also would have to choose the Hanoverians as heirs to the Scottish throne. The Scots would have to start negotiations for a closer union with England or many Scots who had settled in England would be treated as foreigners. Besides, there was also the threat of an English ban on Scottish goods.

The Scots are Stung

Needless to say the Scots were furious. As Lockhart of Carnwath wrote:

> And truly all Scotsmen looked upon it [the Alien Act] as an Invasion of [their] Liberties and Sovereignty, and an insolent Behaviour towards a free and independent People: and 'twas so odd so wise a Nation as England should have been so guilty of so unpolitick [foolish] a Step for they could not have proposed a more effectual Way to irritate the Scots Nation.

Remember, however, that Lockhart was a Jacobite and would have been pleased to see anything that would stir up Scottish resentment against the English and the succession of the Hanoverians.

An English Spy Reports

Still Lockhart was correct in showing the Scots were angry. The English Government had sent several spies to Scotland to report on the situation there. One of these spies was Daniel Defoe, the author of *Robinson Crusoe*, who wrote some clever articles which presented the English point of view to the Scots. Defoe wrote about the Alien Act:

> [It] tended to estrange [make enemies of] the [Scottish] Nation, and so, as it were, prepared them for a Breach, rather than for a Union . . . An Act, in my opinion, the most unpolitic, I had almost said unjust, that ever passed that great Assembly [the English Parliament].

War or Union?

For a time it looked as though war might break out between the two countries. But cooler heads began to take over. They pointed to the second paragraph of the extract in the left-hand column on this page which showed that the English were prepared to negotiate a union. They wrote to Queen Anne saying that the Scottish Estates would not consider sending people to discuss a union with the threat of the Alien Act hanging over their heads. Shortly afterwards, the Alien Act was repealed in the English House of Lords. Commissioners from both countries met to negotiate a union in London.

A Federal Union

The Scots wanted the kind of union in which a Scottish assembly looked after Scottish affairs while a parliament of Great Britain would manage Defence and Foreign Affairs. This federal kind of government is the same as that used in Canada, Australia and the United States today as well as in many other countries. This system of government gives to each federal state the right to raise its own taxes and pass laws which apply only to that state.

An Incorporating Union

The English would have nothing to do with the federal idea. They wanted an 'incorporating' union whereby a united parliament would look after both internal and external matters. The English were not going to take the risk of a Scottish assembly becoming too independent and perhaps trying to break away from the Union which was what the Confederate States did later in America.

Who Was Right?

Perhaps the Scots were ahead of their time. Many different federal governments seem to work well enough and still give the people in each state a certain amount of control over their own affairs. Perhaps the English Commissioners were correct for their time. There was no working system of federal government at that time. They felt they could not get the security they wanted from any other union but an incorporating one.

The Union

In the end the English, as the stronger partner, had their way; though this was managed with a great deal of skill and determination. As Dean Swift, the author of *Gulliver's Travels* put it:

> ... it was thought highly dangerous to leave that Part of the Island inhabited by a poor, fierce Northern People, at Liberty to put themselves under a different King ... and so the Union became necessary, not for the actual Good it could possibly do us, but to avoid a probable Evil.

Parliament Hall in Edinburgh

Cross of St George

Cross of St Andrew

Union Jack

Two flags in one, the Union Jack of 1707

Was Scotland Betrayed?

Why did the incorporating Union pass despite the disapproval of the great majority of the Scottish people? Some historians maintain that promises were made and bribes paid. They point to the actions of the Duke of Hamilton who was leader of the party opposed to union in the Estates. At one time, to the surprise of even the Government's supporters, he allowed the Government to choose the Commissioners who were to negotiate the Union. This made sure that all the Scottish Commissioners supported a Union. At other times Hamilton pushed debates in favour of Union in the Estates—while supposedly totally opposed to Union. Four years after Union was passed in 1707 Hamilton was made Duke of Brandon in the peerage of Great Britain, a strange reward for someone who had been so much against the Union of Great Britain. The Duke of Queensberry, a leading Scottish member of the Government was always seeking rewards for himself. As a Scottish secretary wrote from London in September 1706:

Duke Queensberry . . . said he was not for the Union, etc. but at last a sum of money quieted him. I believe the sum of money is ten thousand pounds; the thing itself is no secret.

An anonymous poem written after the Union entitled, 'Verses on the Scottish Peers 1706' had this to say:

> Our Dukes were de'ills, our Marquesses were
> mad,
> Our Earls were evills, Our Viscounts yet more
> bad,
> Our Lords were villains, and our Barons knaves
> Who with the Burrows [Burghs] did sell us for
> slaves.

The Alternative to Union

One thing that helped the Scottish Commissioners to make up their minds was what might have happened if negotiations had failed. Defoe was not alone when he said that failure would have resulted in war, though he hastened to add that no one would win in such a war. From the English point of view there was no better time to wage a war than after 1706. In that year the Duke of Marlborough had just inflicted another crushing defeat on the French at Ramillies. He was now free to lead an army against the Scots if ordered. The prospect of facing a well-disciplined, victorious army led by one of the greatest generals in history was not relished even by the most patriotic Scot. It lent much weight to the English Commissioners' proposals.

Genuine Desires

You must not think that every Scot who voted for Union did so for bribes or by threats. Many thought that a union was the only way to get rid of the poverty that had plagued Scotland like some evil shadow. To these people there was even more need for a union after the failure of the Darien Scheme.

A Marriage is Arranged

When the Scottish Chancellor Seafield signed the Treaty of Union on 1 May 1707 he turned and said, 'That's the end of an auld sang'. He did so without sadness for he felt the Scots had struck a good bargain. The English, on the other hand, had got their incorporating union and the Hanoverian Succession was assured. Despite many arguments the Scots were only given 45 M.P.s in the united Parliament. A new flag was designed, the Union Jack which incorporated the crosses of St Andrew and St George. Both countries were now to use the same weights and measures as well as the same coinage.

Money, Kirk and Law

The Scots did gain from the Union. They could now trade freely with the English colonies, something the Glasgow merchants seized upon with great success to make their city the second largest in Britain. A sum of £400 000 called the 'Equivalent' was sent to Edinburgh to bring Scotland's public debts into line with England's. People were quick to notice that this sum represented the money lost in the Darien Scheme. Many shareholders who thought they had lost everything were delighted to receive compensation. The 'Equivalent' was not a free gift for the money was to be collected from Scottish taxes. As Sir Walter Scott pointed out in the next century:

> ... in fact, the Parliament of Scotland was bribed with the public money belonging to their own country. In this way Scotland herself was to pay the price given to her legislators [law-givers] for the sacrifice of her independence.

Fears that the Kirk would be destroyed by the Union were set aside when the Kirk was recognised as the official Church of Scotland. The Scots also retained their own legal system.

'How Can I Be Sad on My Wedding Day?'

But was it all worth the loss of Scotland's independence? The Jacobites did not think so, but this was to be expected as the Union was a great obstacle to the return of the Stuarts. News of Jacobite plots with French aid soon began to spread. Most Scots at the time thought that the independence which their ancestors had bought in blood had been sold away. They thought that their beautiful, poor country had been forced into a marriage with the rich but unpopular England. A popular song of the time put it well for most Scots, 'How Can I Be Sad On My Wedding Day?' In England the Union was more welcome. Sir John Clerk was one of the Scottish Commissioners who was very much in favour of Union. He wrote in his Memoirs:

> ... and I reasone to believe that at no time Scotchmen were more acceptable to the English than on that day.

Something to Remember

In 1689 the new independent Scottish Estates found themselves faced with two great problems. The first, the Jacobite threat, was dealt with, for the time being, by the death of Bonnie Dundee at Killiecrankie. The second problem, that of poverty, was greater and more difficult to solve. The Darien Scheme was one attempt to solve it but its failure left the Scots feeling more bitter than ever. Most of this bitterness was directed against the English whom the Scots, rightly or wrongly, regarded as the cause of all their troubles. This bitterness was shown in a number of Scottish actions which caused the English Parliament to hit back so that the threat of war loomed between the two countries.

Despite the difference between the two countries, each needed the other. The Scots needed to trade freely with England and its colonies to break out of the trap of poverty. The English needed the Scots in order to shut off once and for all the threat to England's security which a renewal of the Franco-Scottish Auld Alliance would have brought about. The English felt this need greatly in the middle of a bitter war with France.

It was these mutual needs which finally brought about the Union of 1707. The Union was a marriage of convenience between the English and Scottish nations, stemming from necessity and not love.

Something to Think About

This period in Scottish history brings out very clearly how people think about strangers and foreigners. The Greeks, who had a word for everything, called this 'xenophobia' or 'hatred or fear of foreigners'. This hatred grows stronger the more wealthy and powerful the foreigners are—as the English were to the Scots. Perhaps you can think of some examples of xenophobia today. This mixture of fear and envy often leads to mindless violence, as in the murder of Captain Green. Xenophobia is as much a part of our thinking today as it was in the time of the Union. We should be on our guard against the unthinking feeling of hatred towards foreigners whether they are 'Frenchies', 'Yanks', 'Gerries', 'Argies' or any other kinds of crafty foreigners.

Many people in Scotland feel that the Union should be done away with. They argue that times and conditions have changed in nearly three hundred years. They think that the time has come for the Scots to look after their own affairs again and that they should no longer be ruled by a Government based in London. Opponents of these views think that despite some ups and downs the Union has benefitted both countries. They also say that the Scots have already a large say in their own affairs through the Scottish Office and Scottish Committees in Parliament. Finally, if the Union was done away with, these people fear that the old hostilities between the countries would flare up again. Weigh up the arguments on either side and decide who you think is right.

The Company of Scotland

Great things were expected of the Company of Scotland. The setting-up of a Scottish trading colony on Darien was to make Scotland as successful as the English and the Dutch, the great colonial and trading nations. The fine, solid building that was the Company's headquarters in Edinburgh was a sign of the solid prosperity the Company was to bring to Scotland and its people. Ships were bought and fitted out. Crews were hired and colonists selected—and there was no lack of volunteers. On Thursday 14 July 1698 the *St Andrew* and four other ships set sail with 1200 men, a few women and some boys. The watching crowds at Leith cheered and prayers were said for this brave venture which carried the hopes of Scotland with it: 'so that we may be known to the world to be a nation' as one Scotsman said at the time.

Within a year most of the colonists were dead and the colony abandoned. News took much longer to travel in those days and, ignorant of the fate of the first expedition, another small fleet had set sail from the Clyde in August 1699. Few of these 1300 people ever returned to Scotland for many were buried at Darien or at sea. Of the rest, many sold themselves as slaves to the English colony of Jamaica or became the slaves and prisoners of the Spaniards. The feelings of the second expedition when they arrived at Darien are summed up in a letter from the Company's Directors:

(1)   Edinburgh, the 10th day of February 1700.
GENTLEMEN,
    We know it must needs have been a great disappointment to you as a loss to us, instead of finding, as you expected, a Colony in good condition, well fortified, with houses and other conveniences for your reception and accommodation, or to find only the ruins of a begun settlement, desolate and forsaken by those whose glory it would have been to perish rather than to have abandoned it some shamefully and unaccountably as they did.

Directors to the Officers of the Company

The arms of the Company of Scotland

Darien was not only thought to be a suitable place for trading stations but also a good place for settlers. As one report said:

(2)   Now you may be perswaded that this mortality [deaths] and sicknes did not come by ye unholsomness of ye place or climate; for they all agreed the place is very wholesome, the heat moderate, ye water extraordinary good, and ye soil surpassing belief; all sorts of grain will come to perfection [ripen] 1 month sooner there than any where else.

(*Darien Papers*, ed John Hill Burton, Bannatyne Club. Edinburgh, 1849)

Another report was equally optimistic:

(3)   The place by its situation in this pairt of the world, is fit for commerce; and if money be bestowed, honest men imployed, and good measures followed a firm settlement may be made, so that strangers may promise themselves safely here [newcomers will prosper]: but on planting and improvem'nt [agriculture] no great stress [no promises] can be laid for reimburseing the adventurers, unless negroes be procured, white men being unfitt for that work...

Another letter from Thomas Drummond, one of the officers at Darien seems to completely contradict itself:

> (4) He [Captain Drummond] tells us that their men died and were sick to that height [extent] that the liveing were not able to bury the dead; and that they had not six men for guard and sentries; that all manner of distempers [illnesses], such as head and belly-aches, fevers, fluxes [dysentery], &c [etc], raged among their men; but all this notwithstanding, the place was very wholesome.
>
> (Letter from Council to Directors, 'on board the *Rising Sun*, in Caledonia Bay. 23d December, 1699')

In fact the climate and position of Darien made it one of the unhealthiest places in the world for white people at that time—and for centuries afterwards. It was the breeding-place of tropical diseases of which the worst were Malaria and Yellow Fever. It was not until doctors and scientists had discovered the causes of these diseases which were both passed on to human beings by mosquitoes that the Panama Canal was able to be built at the beginning of this century. The Scots at Darien had no resistance to these diseases and this is one reason for the high number of deaths. A letter by George Moffat from New York where some Scots

landed after the failure of the first expedition is more realistic:

(5) New York, ye 12th Augut. 1699
I am sorry . . . to give an acct. [account] of this sad and tragicall relation of our Scotts Affricane Company's being obliged to leave [New] Caledonia [Darien], not by the force of an enemy of Spaniards, but by that famine and great mortality, which generaly rages together . . .

Spaniards and English

Darien was certainly an excellent position for a trading colony. Unfortunately for the Scots the land was claimed by the Spaniards who resented any other nation trying to set up a colony in the Americas. Worst still, the Scots were Protestant heretics and pirates. In the end the survivors of the second expedition had to surrender to the Spaniards although they were allowed to sail away. Normally, the English would not have cared about the Scots setting up a colony in Spanish territory—though the English did care about any interference with *their* trade. But things were not normal because King William was trying to persuade the Spaniards against a French alliance. A Scottish colony in Spanish territory was the last thing that William wanted. He gave orders to the Governors of the English colonies. Here is part of a Proclamation by Sir William Beeston, Governor of Jamaica, 8 April 1699:

(6) . . . [His Majesty's subjects] do not presume, on any pretence whatever, to hold any correspondence with the said Scots [at Darien], nor to give them any assistance of arms, ammunition, provisions, or any other necessaries whatsoever, either by themselves, or any other for them, or by any of their vessels, or of the English nation, as they will answer the contempt of His Majesty's command to the contrary at their utmost peril.

Note that this Proclamation cut off the Scots from any kind of help from the English although 'His Majesty' King William of England was also 'His Majesty' of Scotland. Much of the suffering of the Scots when they tried to return to their homeland was caused by the severity of these Proclamations.

The Company's Fault?

When both expeditions failed people began to seek those who were to blame and, naturally, no one wanted to admit he had been responsible for so much loss of life, money and pride. There were those who blamed the Company. We should not be surprised that these were the people who returned from Darien. One of them complained that the Company had neglected the colonists:

(7) For its not to be expected that the establishing and carrying on of Collonys abroad can be done without being supplied with men and provisions from home which have all been neglected; for during the time they stayed att Darien, which was about 7 months, they had not ye scratch of a pen.

The Scottish Disease

Disease, the climate, the Spaniards and the English all contributed to the failure of the Darien adventure. What made failure certain was the Scottish disease of quarrelling bitterly among themselves, especially among the leaders of the expedition:

(8) I am informed allso that there was some divisions among ye first elected Councellors, some of them being too hote headed, and oyrs [others] of ym [them] no wayes train'd up to soe great affaires, their agreement . . . was not soe great as was requisite [necessary], many young men of them being swell'd wt. [with] the expectations of their futur and present preferments [offices] . . .

The Directors of the Company had no doubts about the causes of the failure of the first expedition. In a letter to Patrick MacDowall on the ship *Margaret* when she sailed from Leith in March 1700 they stated:

(9) We need not tell you how far the honour and interest of the nation is engaged. There is no looking backward. The disagreements and factious quarelling of your predecessors [members of the first expedition], who were, it seems, void of both religion and morality, will, we hope, be a beacon to you not to split upon the same rock . . . It's a lasting disgrace to the memories of those officers who went on the first expedition, that even the meanest [lowest]

planters were scandalized at the vitiousness [viciousness] of their lives, many of them living very intemperately and vitiously for many months at the publick charge [expense] whilest the most sober [level-headed] and industrious among them were vigilant in doing their duty...

This letter was to be read out to the officers and members of the second expedition at Darien.

It seems as though the second expedition was no better at sticking together than the first. From *The Journals of the Voyage of the Ship 'Margaret'* comes the following lament:

(10) ... that it was no want of provisions obleidged our people to give up Calledonia [Darien], but rather dissention [quarrels] among themselves, with the want of dew conduct and discretion in the manadgers [officers]; and if they had keeped it out [resisted] for some few days longer, the Spaniards had deserted the siedge, both by reason of increasing sickness among them, and the discouradgment they had gott from the arrivall of Captain Drummond, who had come in some few hours after the surrender.

Shades of Glencoe

The Captain Drummond mentioned in the *Journals* had done his fair share of quarrelling at Darien. He had been returning to Scotland to defend his honour when he had met some ships at Jamaica bringing aid to the garrison at Darien. He returned with them and arrived at Darien on 1 April. The previous day the garrison had surrendered to the Spaniards on condition that the Scots were given a fortnight to leave Darien.

You have met Captain Thomas Drummond before. He was the man who brought the fatal orders to Campbell of Glenlyon at Glencoe. During the Massacre Drummond had shot the last of nine bound MacDonald prisoners and a boy of twelve who was begging for mercy at Glenlyon's feet. He was as arrogant, strict and as proud of his family as only the son of a poor Strathearn laird could be.

What Does Darien Show?

The failure of Darien tells us many things about great undertakings. It tells us that enthusiasm and dreams are not enough. Success depends on these and many other things; finding out what difficulties lie ahead and planning to overcome these problems. The planners of Darien either ignored or underestimated these difficulties. Although it must be said that other nations had successfully planted colonies in the Caribbean Sea and South and Central America. Even if they had overcome all these other difficulties, the divisions among their leaders at Darien would probably have doomed the Darien Scheme.

Something you Should Know

Before you come to any conclusions there are some things you ought to know. Perhaps you remember from Book 1 that we should always be very careful about the source of our evidence. When we look at the different sources of evidence for this Case History we must be very careful. Everyone is trying to prove that he is right and those with different ideas are wrong. There is nothing wrong in this as long as we are aware of what is going on. Extracts 3 and 4 were written by members of the Council of the first expedition, *who wanted to prove that Darien was the perfect place for a colony as well as a trading station*, despite the number of deaths. Extracts 2, 5, 7 and 8 were all taken from the *Letters of George Moffat*. Moffat is still convinced that Darien is the ideal place for a settlement but that *the Directors in Edinburgh had not given the first settlers sufficient support*. Also Moffat says that failure was partly due to quarrels amongst the Councillors of the first expedition. The Directors of the Company in Edinburgh have their say in Extracts 1, 9 and 10 where they try to encourage the second expedition *by showing up the bad conduct of the first settlers, especially the leaders of the first expedition*. Notice the Directors say nothing about those who chose the members of the first expedition!

You have to decide who is telling the truth.

A Noble Lord is Executed

On 18 August 1746 Lord Balmerino was led to his execution. He had been found guilty of treason and, as a nobleman, he had the right to be executed by the axe instead of being hanged like any common criminal! Balmerino stepped forward and laid his head upon the block. The executioner leaned forward and whispered to his Lordship that he had placed his head the wrong way on the block and so he would not be able to make a clean job of the beheading. Without a moment's hesitation Balmerino stood up and laid his head correctly on the block. A swift stroke and the brave man was dead.

An 'Anti-Revolutionary' Jacobite

Shortly before his death Balmerino had made a short speech to the on-lookers. He began:

> I was brought up in true, loyal Anti-revolutionary principles [ideas] and I hope the world is convinced that they stick to me. [He ended with a short prayer] 'O Almighty God, I humbly beseech Thee to bless the King, the Prince and the Duke of Yorke, and all the dutiful [rightful] branches of the Royal Family'.

The 'Revolution' that Balmerino was against was the one in 1688 which displaced his 'dutiful' King James VII and II by William and Mary and later on the Hanoverians. As the Latin for 'James' was 'Jacobus', Balmerino and all those who thought like him were called 'Jacobites'.

The Governor of ye Tower delivering the Prisoners to the Sheriffs of London at the Barr for Execution.

London: Printed for Ja. Ryall at Hogarth's head in Fleet Street.

Publish'd According to Act of Parliament.

The View of the Scaffold with the Guards Surrounding at the Time of Execution.

A PERSPECTIVE VIEW of TOWER HILL and the Place of EXECUTION of the LORDS KILMARNOCK and BALMERINO on Monday 18 of August 1746.

'Bonnie Dundee'

We already know that in 1689 there was an attempt to regain the throne of Scotland for James VII. Some of you will know the words of the old song which says Graham of Claverhouse, 'Bonnie Dundee', spoke to the Convention Estates and,

> ... Open the West Port and let us gang free
> For it's up wi' the bonnets o' Bonnie Dundee

Dundee went to the Highlands and soon gathered an army. He was killed in battle and after his death many of the Highlanders returned to their homes. The rest were repulsed at Dunkeld by a tough regiment of Cameron Convenanters. Although James's cause had suffered a set back, many Highland chiefs still regarded him as their true King. It was King William III's doubt about these chiefs' loyalty which led to the Massacre at Glencoe.

The Jacobites and the Union

Many Jacobites were opposed to the Union of 1707. A Jacobite plot the following year came to nothing because a French fleet bringing help to Scottish Jacobites missed the meeting place. However, a number of Jacobites were unwilling to fight against Queen Anne who was the daughter of James II and VII.

When Anne died in 1714 any Jacobite reluctance disappeared for they were all opposed to George I, 'the wee German Lairdie', from Hanover in Germany. He occupied the throne instead of the 'true' James VIII, the son of James VII. The leader of the Scottish Jacobites was the Earl of Mar who had been a supporter of the Union and the Hanoverians until George I refused to give him a high post. Mar immediately became an ardent Jacobite. You can see why he was nicknamed, 'Bobbin' Johnnie'! Mar went north to his estates at Braemar and he persuaded many Highland chiefs and leading men from the north-east to join the cause of 'King James' or 'The Old Pretender' as he came to be called by Hanoverian supporters. Mar hoped for money, arms and soldiers from France, though as he later wrote:

> ... however incredible it may appear ... we never received from Abroad the least supply of Arms or Ammunition of any kind; tho' it was Notorious [well-known] in itself and well-known, both to Friends and Enemies, that this was what from the Beginning we mainly wanted.

The Earl of Mar, 'Bobbin' Johnnie'

Unfortunately for Mar and the other Jacobites in the 1715 Rising, King Louis XIV of France had just died and the new French Government was seeking better relations with Britain.

The '15

A Contrast in Leaders

Mar and the other Jacobite leaders seem to have had no plan except for the rather vague one of joining up with the English Jacobites. They gained a great success when the Jacobites of Perth captured the city and their forces increased to nearly 10 000 men. Success seemed certain for only a small force at Stirling commanded by the Duke of Argyll stood between them and Edinburgh and the South. But victories often depend upon the character of the generals. Mar was a

The Duke of Argyll

Wha Wan at Sheriffmuir?

The two armies met at Sheriffmuir near Dunblane on 13 November 1715. Mar's Highlanders routed a wing of Argyll's infantry but the Government's cavalry swept away the opposite wing of the Jacobite army. Who actually won the battle is a difficult question to answer. In the words of the old song:

> There's some say that we wan,
> And some say that they wan
> And some say that nane wan at a' man.

If it was a drawn battle then Mar lost the campaign for he withdrew his army to Perth.

A Jacobite force under Macintosh of Borlum crossed the Forth and occupied Cromwell's old fort at Leith for a few days before they managed to join with English Jacobites. The two Jacobite forces did not get on well together. Some English cavalry tried

diplomat and good at making rousing speeches. His great talent lay, as Lockhart of Carnwath wrote:

> . . . in the cunning management of his designs [plans] and projects in which was hard to find him out, when he aimed to be incognito [not found out].

Mar's cunning contrasted with the Duke of Argyll of whom Lockhart also wrote:

> . . . he was extremely forward in effecting what he aimed at and designed, which he owned and promoted above board, being altogether free of the least share of dissimulation [deceit], and his word so sacred that one might assuredly depend upon it . . .

Argyll was also a good soldier who had received his training under Marlborough. He did not have a great deal of confidence in his own troops when facing Highlanders, for as he said:

> A Lamb is not more afraid of a Lyon, than these Low Countrey [Lowland] people are of the Highlanders.

Though we must remember that Argyll was a Highlander himself.

CHIEF INCIDENTS OF THE JACOBITE RISING IN SCOTLAND (1715) — THE MARCH ON PERTH; BATTLE NEAR DUNBLANE; ATTEMPT UPON THE CASTLE OF EDINBURGH, ETC.
From "Prints after Louis du Guernier" (1917-12-8-1151), *in the British Museum.*

to force the Highlanders to fight in England:

> Whereupon the Highlanders cocked their fire-locks and said, if they were to be made a sacrifice, they would choose to have it done in their own country.

The Old Pretender

On 22 December the Old Pretender landed at Peterhead. By this time the Jacobites were quarrelling among themselves and the Highlanders were deserting. The Old Pretender was a cold, shy man not the sort of person for whom men would fight and die for. As an unknown Jacobite wrote:

> I must not conceal that when we saw the Person who we called our King, we found ourselves not at all animated [excited] by his Presence, and if he was disappointed in us, we were tenfold more in him.

After two months he boarded a ship at Montrose for France. From there he settled down in Rome and never went on his travels again. Thirty years were to pass before another royal Stuart landed in Britain. The '15 Rebellion had a good chance of success in the beginning but failed through the lack of good and decisive leadership.

The '45

In 1745 Britain and France were at war again. Prince Charles Edward Stuart, the elder son of the Old Pretender, tried to persuade the French to send an expedition to Britain under his leadership. Though they were impressed by the enthusiasm of the 25-year-old Prince, the French were not prepared to waste men and money on what they considered a wild gamble. Finally, Charles became so frustrated by the inaction that he set sail for Scotland with a few friends. They reached Eriskay on 23 July. A few days later he sent messages from Moidart to the Jacobite chiefs asking them to join his standard. One of them, Cameron of Lochiel, saw how few men Charles had and advised him to return to France. Charles replied:

> In a few days, with the few friends I have, I will erect the royal standard, and proclaim to the people of Britain that Charles Stuart is come to claim the Crown of his ancestors, to win it or perish in the attempt. Lochiel, who, my father has often told me, was our firmest friend, may stay at home and learn from the newspapers the fate of his Prince.
> 'No', said Lochiel, 'I'll share the fate of my Prince; and so shall every man whom nature or fortune have given me power.'

James Edward Stuart, the 'Old Pretender'

Donald Cameron of Lochiel

The Power of the Chief

Lochiel was not boasting when he said all his clans-men would follow him. An English officer, Captain Burt, had visited the Highlands earlier in the century and had this to say about the clansman's loyalty to his chief:

> . . . the ordinary Highlander esteem it the most sublime degree of virtue to love their chief and pay him a blind obedience, although it is opposi-tion to the government, the laws of the king-dom, or even the laws of God. He is their idol: and as they profess to know no king but him . . . so will they say, they ought to do whatever he commands without enquiry [question].

Burt got only part of the truth. The chief was the father of the 'clann', which means 'children' in Gaelic; for he was the descendant of the person who had founded the clan. Like a family the clan followed the chief to war or when he led them on a cattle raid. At these times the chief called upon his 'tacksmen', who were often close relatives, to bring their men to the battlefield. In this way the greatness of the clan de-pended upon how many men the chief could lead into battle.

Beneath the tacksmen were the clansmen whose position depended upon the amount of land they farmed or cattle they possessed. The lowest men were called 'cottars' who often farmed less than a hec-tare and many cottars even had servants whose only land was a potato-strip or piece of one. If a clansman or cottar did not obey his chief's orders to go to war then his cottage might be burned down as a punish-ment. The tacksmen were ruthless in obeying the chief's orders.

How the Clansman Fought

The clansman was a superb fighting soldier trained in the use of broadsword, dirk and target or shield from the time he was a child. This is what the Jacobite Chevalier de Johnstone said of their way of fighting:

> Their manner of fighting is adapted for brave but indisciplined men. They advance with rapidity, discharge their pieces [fire their guns] when within musket-length of the enemy . . . Having got within the bayonets, and into the ranks of the enemy . . . the fate of the battle is decided in an instant, and the carnage [blood-shed] follows; the Highlanders bringing down two men at a time, one with the dirk in the left hand, and another with a sword.

It was even more difficult for a normal, slow moving army of the time to catch a Highland army. The Highlander could move over the roughest of country and live on the barest of food, often no more than a pouch of oatmeal. If he could not find shelter he would wrap himself in his plaid and sleep soundly in the coldest and wettest of weather. We have already seen what the Lowlander thought of the Highlander, but what about the other way round? This is what General Wade said:

> They have still a more extensive adherence [have more in common] one to another as Highlanders in opposition to the people who Inhabit the Low Countries, whom they hold in the utmost Con-tempt, imagining them inferior to themselves in Courage, Resolution and the use of Arms. . .

The Anti-Jacobite Clans

Not all the clans were Jacobite. The powerful Clan Campbell fought on the Hanoverian side. In some cases if a chief followed Charles he would send one of his sons to fight for the Hanoverians. In this way, whatever happened, the clan would be on the win-ning side, or so they hoped. So two Chisholm brothers faced each other on opposing sides in the later battle of Culloden. There were even two Dukes of Atholl fighting each other in the '45. The elder brother had been a Jacobite in 1715 and had been stripped of his title which had been given to his youn-ger brother. Now in 1745 the two Dukes were again on opposite sides.

Why Some Chiefs Chose Charles

Still, many Highland chiefs fought for the Jacobite cause in 1745. You have already seen why some chose to do this but there were other reasons. Some re-sented the building of Government forts in the High-lands which restricted their power. Others felt that the growth of Lowland laws and customs were a threat to their authority. If these chiefs restored the Stuarts then they thought their authority would be maintained.

The Jacobite Army Grows

When the clan chiefs heard that Lochiel had decided to follow Charles most of them joined the Jacobite force. There were chiefs like MacDonald of Clanra-nald and the Frasers under their crafty old chief, Simon Fraser of Lovat. Simon Fraser had been on the

Government's side in the '15. In a few weeks the Jacobite army numbered about 2400 men.

Sir John Cope Moves into Action

When Sir John Cope Commander of the Government's forces in Scotland heard how many chiefs had joined Charles he marched north to crush the rising before it could spread. He reached the Corrieyairack Pass which led to Fort Augustus but when he heard of a large Jacobite army, Cope decided to march to Inverness and ship his army back to Leith. Faced with no opposition the Jacobites moved swiftly and captured Perth on 4 September. There the Jacobites spent a week being drilled by Lord George Murray, a fine soldier, who, according to the Chevalier de Johnstone:

> ... possessed a genius for military operations ... tall and robust, and brave in the highest degree ... conducting the Highlanders in the most heroic manner ... always the first to rush sword in hand into the midst of the enemy ...

Edinburgh Captured

Inspired by Charles who wore the Highland dress and marched with his men, the Jacobites soon captured Linlithgow. On 16 September the Highlanders had their first taste of battle. At Coltbridge, on the outskirts of Edinburgh, a small group of Highlanders fired a few shots at a force of Government cavalry which galloped off in panic. On the following day Lochiel and his men hid near one of the gates to the city and when it was opened for a coach they rushed in and took the capital. Charles led a victory parade into the city and set up his court in Holyrood Palace where his grandfather had once stayed. Even a few cannon shots fired from the Castle which had not surrendered did not mar the Jacobite victory celebrations.

Battle of Prestonpans

When Cope discovered that the Jacobites had captured Edinburgh, he sailed to Dunbar where he disembarked his troops. As he was marching towards the city Cope received news that the Jacobite army was approaching and took up a strong position near Prestonpans. Cope was reluctant to meet the Highlanders in a pitched battle because his army was in poor shape. Many of his men were terrified by the tales of the Highlanders' fierceness. Cope's position was protected by a marsh on one side and by the sea on the other. He was satisfied that he could not be taken by surprise.

Unfortunately for Cope, a local gentleman showed the Highlanders a safe way through the marsh which they silently crossed during the night. Cope was awakened by the horrific sight of the Jacobites lined up and waiting to charge. He tried to move his army to cope with this threat but at this moment the Highlanders charged. This is how an officer in Cope's army described what happened:

> They came on with furiows precipitation [speed]. This disconcerted [upset] all the poor general's dispositions [arrangements] and he was in surprise and confusion ... The Highland troups battells [forces] came on so furiowsly that they were in, sword in hand. The dragoons [cavalry] ran off at the first fire.

Lord George Murray

General Cope flees to Dunbar

The Jacobites later said that the battle had lasted for only eight minutes and they lost only thirty-four men. The Jacobites were delighted and many songs were written to celebrate their victory. Some of you may know one that was written much later by Robert Burns which begins:

Hey Johnnie Cope are ye waukin' yet,
Or are you sleepin' I would wit [think] . . .

Return to Edinburgh

Charles returned to Edinburgh to celebrate his victory. He seemed to be master of Scotland with his invincible Highlanders. In fact, there were large areas of Scotland, including Glasgow, which still strongly supported the Government. More recruits joined the Jacobites but Charles thought he would receive many more from the north-west of England. Indeed, Charles believed all along that no Briton would fight against the 'true' King, his father. When after six weeks the Jacobites marched south it had about 6000 infantry and 500 cavalry. The Government had reacted swiftly to the news from Prestonpans and troops had been brought back from the Continent. Soon there were two powerful armies facing the Jacobites; one at Newcastle under Marshal Wade and another marching from London.

A nineteenth-century painting of Charles Edward Stuart, the 'Young Pretender' at Holyrood House

Advance and Retreat

On 1 November the Jacobites marched south. In order to trick Wade they marched to Kelso and then swung swiftly south-west to Carlisle. The town and castle surrendered to the Jacobites because:

> The dread the inhabitants had of a siege, together with the cowardice of the militia [local troops], made them hang out a white flag, the 14th November.

It was said that mothers hid their children because they had heard the Highlanders were cannibals! As they marched further south few recruits joined the Jacobites. Thirty years is a long time for any cause to remain powerful in people's memories. Charles received more bad news when he heard that volunteers had flocked to the Government's cause in Scotland. Worse still, a powerful army under the Duke of Cumberland, George II's son, was approaching from the south. Despite all this, Charles hoped to capture London by a bold march and the Jacobite army reached Derby on 4 December.

'Black Friday'

In spite of the fire-works and celebrations which greeted their arrival, the Jacobite chiefs and generals feared they were marching into a trap where they would be outnumbered four to one in hostile country. Desertions were increasing in their army for the men were tired and ill-equipped. One hostile English observer had this to say of the Highlanders:

> . . . most of their main body a parcel of shabby, lousy, pitiful-looking fellows, mixed up with old men and boys; dressed in dirty plaids, and as dirty shirts, without breeches . . . and some without shoes, or next to none, and numbers of them so fatigued with their long march, that they really commanded our pity rather than our fear.

A Council of War met and all except Charles were for a retreat to Scotland:

> The Prince heard these words with the greatest of impatience, fell into a passion [temper] and gave most of the Gentlemen that had Spoke very Abusive Language and said they had a mind to betray him.

When he realised that he was not going to have his way Charles became very gloomy and sulky, refusing to have anything to do with the retreat. All the arrangements were left to Lord George Murray whom Charles regarded as the leader of the revolt.

From now on relations between the two men became very strained which had a bad effect on the army.

Panic in London

Perhaps they might have pressed on if they had known the terror in London caused by the Jacobite advance. In London a Jacobite agent said:

> All the merchants shut their doors . . . Everyone ran on the bank for the payment of their notes . . . and expected to see our [Jacobite] army, in two or three days enter London in triumph. King George [II] made all his yachts come with speed to the Tower causing them to embark [load] on board all that he had most precious, and order them to hold themselves ready to depart at a moment's notice.

It remains one of the great 'ifs' of history what would have happened if the Jacobites had pushed on to London.

Glasgow Punished

But the decision had been taken, though most of the clansmen when they found:

> We were retracing our steps, we heard nothing but howling, groans and lamentations . . .

The Government armies were in hot pursuit and only the skill of Murray brought the Jacobites safely back to Scotland on 20 December. They retreated through Glasgow which was fined £5500 and many supplies for supporting the Government:

> The Prince resolved to Punish the Town of Glasgow, who showed a little too much Zelle [zeal] to the Government in raising their militia.

Falkirk

The retreat continued to Falkirk through Stirling where the Jacobites tried vainly to capture the castle. General Hawley, who had replaced Cope said:

> I do and always shall despise these Rascalls . . . the most despicable Enemy that are . . .

At Falkirk Hawley was so contemptuous of the Highlanders that he ordered his cavalry to attack without the support of the infantry. The cavalry charge was stopped:

> . . . so much, that the English cavalry rushed through their own infantry in the battlefield behind them; there it immediately fell into disorder and dragged their army with them in full rout.

Hawley was so upset by the behaviour of his men that he hanged some on the gallows he had prepared for the Jacobites. Shortly afterwards he wrote:

> I never saw any troops in platoons fire more regularly, ... or attack with more bravery and better order, than those Highlanders did at the battle of Falkirk.

It is interesting the things that make people change their minds. Cumberland realised that different ways of fighting would have to be used to defeat the Highlanders.

Retreat to Culloden

The Jacobite retreat to the Highlands continued. Supplies, always a weak point, began to run short. The men were exhausted by the constant marching with the enemy close on their heels. On 15 April Cumberland reached Nairn and received news that the Jacobites were in Inverness. When the Jacobites heard the news that Cumberland was celebrating his twenty-fifth birthday they planned a night-attack hoping to catch the Government as 'drunk as beggars'. The attackers reached Cumberland's camp at dawn when it was too late for a surprise attack and the Highland army retreated to Culloden Moor in an exhausted and hungry condition.

In this painting of the Battle of Culloden the artist used Jacobite prisoners as his models

The Battle of Culloden

The Government army appeared, fresh, well-supplied and out-numbering the Jacobites by about three to one. In fact there were more Scotsmen in Cumberland's army than in Charles's, so we cannot call the '45 a war between the 'Scots' and the 'English'. The open, wind-swept moor gave the Highlanders no protection against Cumberland's cannon and cavalry. Lord George Murray wrote:

> Not a single souldier but would have been against such a field had their advice been askt. A plain [flat] moor where regular troops had full use of their cannons so as to annoy [torment] the Highlanders prodigiously [greatly] before they could make an attack.

You can gather what Murray thought of the choice of battlefield by General O'Sullivan who had just been appointed to command the army by Charles.

Murray was correct about the Government cannon for as the Highlanders stood waiting for the order to charge they were raked with cannon shot with great loss of life. After a few feeble attempts the Jacobite gunners gave up trying to reply. In desperation the left wing of the Highlanders charged without orders. The Government's gunners changed to grapeshot which swept the Highlanders mercilessly. The left and centre of the Jacobite army swerved to the right to escape the grapeshot and hampered the Jacobite right wing in doing so. When they finally reached Cumberland's infantry they found them drawn up in three lines which enabled the back lines to shoot over the heads of the kneeling front line while it was reloading.

With amazing courage the Highlanders pressed on and some managed to break into the left flank of Cumberland's lines. There the Highlanders received another shock. Cumberland had trained his men to use the bayonet on the enemy to their right, so that, when the Highlander raised his broadsword to strike he left his left side unprotected against the bayonet's stab. The Highlanders reeled back and were caught in a flanking fire from some Campbell troops who were firing from behind a stone wall on the Jacobites' right. Cumberland ordered his cavalry to charge. The Highland army began to break up. Charles was hurried away to safety. Cumberland's cavalry pursued the fleeing Highlanders to Inverness killing innocent people as well as their beaten enemy. A Hanoverian supporter wrote:

> ... the moor was covered in blood: and our own men what with the killing the enemy, dabbling their feet in the blood; and splashing it about one another looked like so many butchers.

Butcher Cumberland

Cumberland said that he discovered a Jacobite order that Government troops were to be shown no mercy. He reminded his troops of this order—which proved to be a forgery—when he sent them to deal with the Jacobite wounded and prisoners after the battle. Wounded Highlanders on the Moor were shot, clubbed or bayonetted to death. When prisoners were not killed they were put in prisons without care or medical supplies. Many died there and the rest were executed or transported. For his orders after the battle Cumberland received the nickname which has stuck to him—'Butcher Cumberland'.

The End of the Clans

The '45 had badly frightened the British Government and it was determined to prevent any further Jacobite risings. Troops ranged the Highlands tracking down Jacobite fugitives, burning, looting and killing on their way. Typical of this behaviour was an order by General Bland to the commander of the troops sent to demolish Lochiel's house:

> ... to destroy as many of them as he can, since prisoners would only embarrass him [be an inconvenience]; and in case the country people did not come in immediately, deliver up their arms, and submit to the King's mercy, he was to burn and destroy their habitations, seize all their cattle, and put the men to death, being pretty well assured it will be difficult for him to shed innocent blood on that account.

Over 120 Jacobites were executed, including Lord Balmerino and Simon Fraser. Most Highland chiefs fled to exile in France and their lands were confiscated. Laws were passed which took away their power over their clansmen. Highlanders were forbidden to carry weapons or play the bagpipes which were considered a weapon of war. They were not allowed to wear the kilt which the Government also considered a military uniform! The clans were broken up. The Gaelic language, poetry and music were regarded with suspicion. The Gaelic poet, Roy Stewart, who had fought at Culloden lamented:

Woe is me for the host of the tartan.
Scattered and spread everywhere . . .

Less than thirty years later the Englishman Dr Johnson said this of the people of the west coast:

The clans retain now little of their original character: their ferocity of temper is softened, their military ardour is extinguished, their dignity of independence is depressed, and contempt of government subdued, and their reverence for their chiefs abated. Of what they had before the late conquest of their country there remains only their language and their poverty.

Charles after Culloden

Prince Charles escaped to France after many adventures. After Culloden a reward of £30 000 was put on his head but he was never betrayed. Many of the worst atrocities that followed Culloden were committed by Lowland Scot upon Highland Scot but Charles showed little interest in the fate of the Highlanders. He returned to Rome where he died a lonely and disappointed old man on 30 January 1788, on the same day 139 years after his great-grandfather, Charles I was executed. In the end, the Highlanders were greater than the cause for which they had suffered and died. They, and not the House of Stuart, were the real heroes.

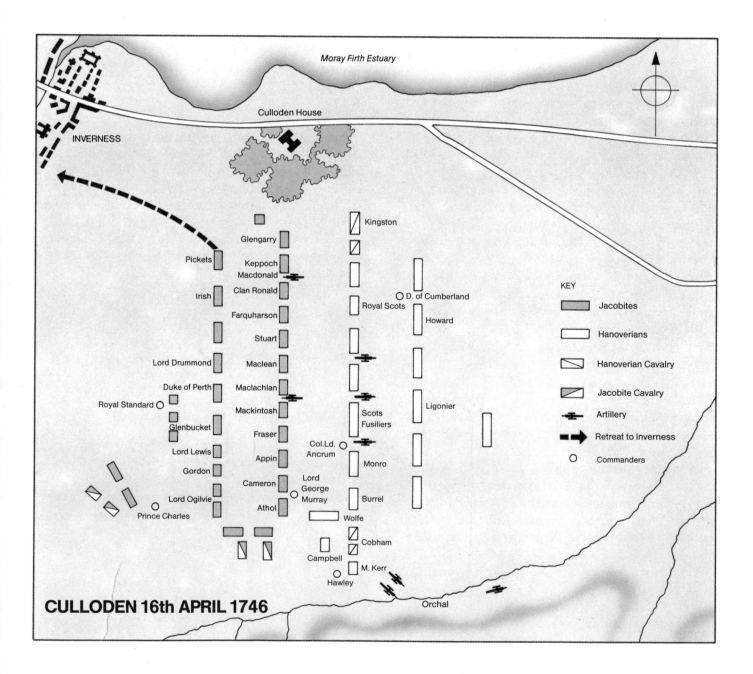

CULLODEN 16th APRIL 1746

Something to Remember

Notice the reasons people had for joining the Jacobite cause. Some did it for high ideals; they believed the Stuarts were appointed by God to rule and that no human could change that. Many Catholics joined because the Stuarts were Catholics. Many Scots fought for the Stuarts because they regarded the Stuarts as Scots. Some Jacobites just hated England and the Union of 1707. Some Highland chiefs thought the only way to retain their power was by a Stuart Restoration.

After the Union it became obvious that no Parliament would restore the Stuarts. The only way to achieve this was by arms. The Highland chiefs were the only people who could supply a ready-made army and this is why both the '15 and '45 began in the Highlands. The Jacobites suffered from poor leadership in both risings with the exception of Lord George Murray from whom Prince Charles took away the leadership at a vital moment. The main reason for the Jacobite victories was the fighting qualities of the Highland clansmen. The main reasons for its defeat were poor leadership and the overwhelming Government force of men and weapons.

Perhaps the most important reason why the Jacobites failed was because they did not get the support of the mass of the British people. Many in Scotland and England regarded the Stuarts with suspicion because of their religion. Many others feared that the restoration of the Stuarts would also mean a royal dictatorship. In Scotland, because the Stuarts relied upon the Highlanders, they lost the support of those Lowlanders who feared and detested the Jacobite clansmen.

Something to Think About

The Jacobite wars show us the best and worst in human beings. They show how people are willing to suffer great hardships and even death for a cause they believe in. Lord Balmerino is only one example of those who died for their beliefs. Many Highland clansmen died because they thought it was their duty to follow their chief without question. On both sides many fought to preserve their way of life. Both then and now, those who were fighting overlooked the suffering they inflicted upon innocent people.

Fear brings out the worst in people. This is clearly seen when British soldiers murdered wounded Highlanders after Culloden. And these atrocities were followed up by others. Both the British Government and Government soldiers had been given a great fright by the Jacobite victories. They were determined to prevent any further risings and rooted out the clans who supplied the Jacobite fighting power. In doing so they rooted out a system which had lasted for thousands of years. They nearly destroyed the Highlanders' language and did destroy their way of life. In destroying the clans they nearly destroyed the people. Racial hatred was shown by the killing of Scot by Scot for the Lowlander regarded the Highlander as a highly dangerous foreigner who happened to live in the same country.

The Legend of Bonnie Prince Charlie

'Bonnie Prince Charlie' as a young man

The legends about Prince Charles Edward Stuart began from the moment he stepped on Scottish soil in 1745 and have persisted down to the present day. Some legends see him as the 'Young Chevalier'; brave, bold, loved by all who met him. This hero was adored by all those who took part in the great adventurous cause of winning back the throne of Britain for the Stuarts. Among those who thought this was Lord Balmerino. He said just before his execution:

> I must beg leave to tell you the incomparable sweetness of his [Charles's] nature, his compassion, his justice, his temperance [moderation], his patience, and his courage are virtues seldom to be found in one person. In short he wants no qualifications requisite to make a great man.

It is difficult to believe that this Charles is the same person who escaped from Culloden without a word of gratitude for those who had fought and died for him. Afterwards, he showed no concern for the fate of those who suffered at the hands of the redcoats. When he entered Edinburgh in triumph in 1745 women flung the white roses of the Jacobites before his horse. Perhaps it is just as well that they could not peer into the future and see Charles when he died in 1788—a pathetic, friendless drunkard. He quarrelled with Lord George Murray at the capture of Carlisle and was furious with the Highland chiefs who supported Murray's decision to retreat from Derby. He sulked on the retreat to Scotland. Charles chose Culloden as a battlefield, despite the pleas of Murray and Lochiel. His choice was to prove a bloody disaster for his followers. Yet these are undoubtedly the same person. But what caused the change? Perhaps the modern historian, Sir Charles Petrie, points to the main reason when he wrote:

> . . . he [Charles] was incapable of resisting the soul-destroying effects of failure.
>
> (Sir Charles Petrie, *The Jacobite Movement*, Eyre & Spottiswoode, 1959, p. 452.)

The moment of failure, when he could not persuade people to follow him and his cause, was not at Culloden, but at Derby. He was convinced that the throne of his ancestors was within his grasp, and perhaps he was correct. The Highland chiefs had deserted him, the 'true' Prince, and disloyalty was something he could never forgive. In this way Charles was a true Stuart. If he had ever felt loyalty in return, it probably left him at Derby. Charles lived for forty-two years after Derby. It is probably true that he felt a failure after Derby and everything that happened afterwards confirmed his feelings. Twenty-five is too young to be a failure. Many years later Charles was visited by an English visitor. Charles's daughter Charlotte came into the room and found her father in a fit. She turned angrily to the visitor saying:

> O Sir, what is this? You must have been speaking to my father about Scotland and the highlands. No one dares to mention these subjects in his presence.

Charles Edward Stuart
as an old man

The Legend is Created

During the '45 Rebellion Charles did a great deal to start his own legend. However, Robert Forbes, the Episcopalean Bishop of Ross and Cromarty, was the person who forged the legend of Bonnie Prince Charlie for future generations. Forbes was an ardent Jacobite who was on his way to join his Prince when he was arrested and imprisoned in Stirling Castle. He spent the rest of the '45 there but he met other Jacobite prisoners who told him of Charles's hardships and adventures after Culloden. Forbes wrote down all these tales in ten black bound notebooks which he entitled 'The Lyon in Mourning'. He kept adding to his notebooks almost up to his death in 1775.

Charles could not have asked for a better person to create his legend. Every little detail is lovingly recorded there. Anything that would reflect badly on the Prince is neglected or glossed over. When Charles has been drinking heavily it is recorded, almost with awe, that he is still standing apparently unaffected while his drinking companions lie under the table. In later life, Bishop Forbes refused to listen to or speak ill of his Prince. When tales of Charles's wild life reached Scotland from abroad Forbes and his fellow-Jacobites blamed everyone else—Charles's Irish friends, the French, the English—everyone except Charles.

Future Generations

Forbes and his companions in the Jacobite Cause did well by their Prince. In 1788, the future Sir Walter Scott met a Jacobite named Stuart who was dressed in mourning. When Scott asked him if a relative had died, he replied: 'No, I am mourning for my poor chief.' These Jacobites passed on the stories of Prince Charles to their children who were given Jacobite names. The Laird of Gask, who had been 'out' in the '45, named his daughter Carolina after Charles. Carolina Oliphant turned out to be a fine poetess. She wrote Jacobite lyrics to fit old Scottish tunes for her uncle, Duncan Robertson of Struan. Later, Carolina married into another Jacobite family and became Lady Nairne. She is the person who wrote the words to many famous Jacobite songs such as 'Charlie Is My Darling', 'The Hundred Pipers' and 'Will Ye No' Come Back Again?'

Jacobite Poets

There are at least three other versions of 'Charlie Is My Darling', one composed by Robert Burns and the other by James Hogg, 'The Ettrick Shepherd'. Yet Burns was a democrat and supported the French Revolution and the ideas of the equality of men. It seems strange that the poet who wrote 'A Man's a Man for A' That' also wrote ballads in honour of a Prince and a Cause which he probably would have fought against, if he had been alive during the '45.

A People in Search of a Hero

After 1746 the Jacobite Cause grew weaker and weaker with the passing years. Strangely enough, the legend of Prince Charlie grew stronger and stronger. It grew even stronger after his death. Much of this was due to the poems and songs of people like Lady Nairne and Burns. There were other causes also. After the Union of 1707 power went south to London. Edinburgh ceased to have any political power and Scotland was neglected. The English had been worried about Jacobite plots coming from north of the Border and had been frightened by the near-success of the '45. For many years after 1746 the Scots, *all Scots* not just the Highlanders, were mistrusted by the English. This made the Scots resentful especially as many thought they had not received any great benefit from the Union.

All the while English influence was growing. In order to better themselves, many Scots got rid of their 'Scottish' accent as best they could. 'Proper' English manners were in; 'uncouth' Scottish ones were out. The Scots looked for ways to resist this English invasion. One way was to go back to 'auld' Scotland, to an independent Scotland and search for a 'Scottish' hero. And there were plenty of them; Wallace, Bruce and Prince Charles. As a Scottish historian, John Hill Burton, put it at the beginning of this century:

> A people imaginative, national and gifted with song, are ever on the watch for any stray hero, and when they find him they have a curious self-deceptive attitude [they deceive themselves] for discovering he is the hero of their own cause.

Hill Burton was referring to Prince Charles when he wrote these words.

By adopting Charles as one of their heroes, Scots were able to show they were different from the English. Later on Sir Walter Scott made the Highlanders romantic heroes—Scottish romantic heroes. This and the example of King George IV led many Lowland Scots to wear the costume of the Highlander—the kilt. This was something which their ancestors would have died rather than have worn. But the kilt soon became accepted in the imagination as being the national dress of the Scots. Very soon afterwards the kilt-makers began making tartans for clans which had never existed—but 'Scotsmen' felt they had to have clans, kilts and tartans if they were to be different from Englishmen.

Dark Satanic Mills

By the beginning of the nineteenth century many Scots, like Sir Walter Scott, hated the spread of industries with their 'dark, satanic mills'. Hating their present, they went back to a simpler and better past, as they thought. It was a past when a man was loyal to his Prince—and what better Prince than Charlie? This nostalgia for a better past was a great help to the growing legend of Prince Charlie.

Those Who Left, Never to Return

Many of the Jacobite songs were about those who had to flee into exile. In his song, 'It Was A' for Our Rightfu' King' Burns wrote:

> It was a' for our rightfu' King
> We left fair Scotland's strand;
> It was a' for our rightfu' King,
> We e'er saw Irish land, my dear
> We e'er saw Irish land.

This homesickness was being felt in the early nineteenth century by thousands of Scots who were leaving their homeland to settle in the new lands overseas; in Canada, the U.S.A., Australia and such like. One 'Jacobite' poem written by Allan Cunningham who was born in 1784, captured the feelings of those who left and those who remained behind:

> Hame, hame, hame, O hame fain wad I be—
> O hame, hame, hame, to my ain countree.

It was for these reasons that the leader of a lost cause was to remain the romantic hero in Scottish legend. It would have suited the legend better if Charles had died at bayonet's point at Culloden. If he had been captured after his wanderings in the heather and then died heroically on the axeman's block like his grandfather Charles I or his great-great grandmother Mary, then a fine note of tragedy would have been added to his legend. He did not, and so the legend quietly obscures all that happened to him after he escaped to France in 1746.

Scottish Country Life at the Time of the '45

At the time of the '45 most of the Scottish people lived in the country and gained their living by farming. The 'ferm-toun' or village was the centre of farming activities. Most of the houses were made of stones, 'divots' or turfs, wood, clay and wattle [branches].

The fields around the toun were divided into in-fields and outfields. The infield was nearer the village and the land was cultivated all the time. A part of the outfield would be farmed for a few years and the villagers would move to another part when the soil became exhausted. The fields were ploughed in ridges or run-rigs and each villager received a different number scattered among the fields.

Oats and barley-bere were the two main crops. The first was for food and the latter for making a kind of ale. The poor methods of farming meant that the villagers were rarely able to produce more than enough to eat, to provide seed for the following year and to pay the rent to the laird or local landlord.

We must remember that the methods of farming had remained almost unchanged for centuries. The same unchanging pattern also applied to the lives of the villagers and their housing. After the '45 changes which had started before the rising began to take place. These changes were to completely transform farming and the life of farming people.

'The soil is much the same for some space either north or south [of the Border], but the fences, enclosures and agriculture are not at all alike. The English are clean and laborious, and the Scotch excessively lazy and dirty, though far short indeed, of what we found at a greater distance from the borders.'

(Colonel James Wolfe, in a letter to his mother, *c.* 1750)

'[I forced my] Tennants at Pennicuik to divide their Lands, for till now all of them were in Run-Rig. This I found a very difficult matter, for that few Tennants could be induced [persuaded] to alter their bad methods of Agriculture.'

(Sir John Clerk of Penicuik. *c.* 1730)

'The claitier [dirtier] the heartier.'
(Old Scottish saying)

'The vulgar [belonging to the common people] houses and what are seen in the villages are low and feeble. Their walls are made of a few stones jumbled together without mortar to cement 'em, on which they set up pieces of wood meeting at the top, ridge-fashion, but so ordered that there is neither sightliness nor strength ... they cover these houses with turff of an inch thick and in the shape of larger tiles which they fasten with wooden pins and renew as often as there is occasion; and that is frequently done. 'Tis rare to find chimneys in these places, a small vent in the roof sufficing to convey the smoake away.'

(Thomas Morer, *A short account of Scotland ... c.* 1689)

'Three years oot an' ane year in
Will keep a field in guid heart till the De'il gangs blin'.
(Old Scottish folk saying)

'ane to gnaw an' ane to saw
An' ane to pay the laird witha.'
(Old Scottish saying about their yield of crops)

'... These pladds [plaids] are about seven or eight yards long, [6.8m] differing in fineness according to the abilities [richness] or fancy of the wearers. They [the Highlanders] cover the whole body with 'em from the neck to the knees, excepting the right arm, which they mostly keep at liberty [free]. Many of them have nothing under these garments besides waistcoats and shirt, which descend no lower than the knee, and they so gird [wrap] 'em about the middle as to give 'em the same length as the linen under 'em, and therefore supply the defect of drawers and breeches.'
(Thomas Morer, *A Short Account of Scotland* *c.* 1689)

Their [the Lowlanders] habit [clothes] is mostly English, saving that the meaner [poorer] sort of men wear bonnets instead of hats, and pladds instead of cloaks; when they go abroad [out of doors], either to market or church. They cover both body and head with 'em, and are so contrived [designed] to be at once both a scarf and a hood.'
(Thomas Morer, *A Short Account of Scotland* *c.* 1689)

'The chearfu' supper done, wi' serious face,
They round the ingle [hearth] form a circle wide,
The Sire [father] turns o'er wi' patriarchal [fatherly] grace,
The big ha' [family] Bible, ance [once] his Father's pride.'
(Robert Burns, 'The Cottar's Saturday-night')

101

Index